BASIC LETTER & MEMO WRITING

FOURTH EDITION
INSTRUCTOR'S MANUAL

Susie H. VanHuss, Ph. D.
Professor and Program
Director of Management
University of South Carolina
Columbia, South Carolina

JOIN US ON THE INTERNET
WWW: http://www.thomson.com
EMAIL: findit@kiosk.thomson.com   A service of I(T)P®

South-Western Educational Publishing
an International Thomson Publishing company I(T)P®

Cincinnati • Albany, NY • Belmont, CA • Bonn • Boston • Detroit • Johannesburg • London • Madrid
Melbourne • Mexico City • New York • Paris • Singapore • Tokyo • Toronto • Washington

Vice President of Publishing	Peter McBride
Production Coordinator	Patricia M. Boies
Manufacturing Coordinator	Kathy Hampton
Marketing Manager	Mark Linton
Marketing Coordinator	Tricia Allen
Cover Design	Lou Ann Thesing

Copyright © 1998

by SOUTH-WESTERN EDUCATIONAL PUBLISHING

Cincinnati, OH

ISBN: 0-538-67520-9

4 5 6 7 8 9 PN 05 04 03 02 01 00

Printed in the United States of America

I**T**P®
International Thomson Publishing

CONTENTS

CHAPTER 10   EMPLOYMENT COMMUNICATIONS

APPENDICES

TRANSPARENCY MASTERS

PREFACE

WRITE EFFECTIVELY

Students must acquire the ability to communicate effectively in writing if they are to be successful in their educational endeavors and in their careers. *Basic Letter and Memo Writing, 4th edition,* is designed to help students become more effective writers by

- Enhancing their writing style by adapting their basic style to meet the needs of the reader and the particular situation.
- Employing good strategies for solving business problems.
- Learning and using effective editing techniques.
- Developing information management skills and using technology effectively to facilitate writing and production of messages.
- Becoming more aware of cultural diversity and the importance of the global marketplace.

APPLY CRITICAL THINKING TO THE WRITING PROCESS

Effective writing incorporates many subskills, such as analyzing, visualizing, and decision making. These subskills are emphasized in *Basic Letter and Memo Writing.*

The reason for producing a document often determines the specific subskills needed to prepare an effective document. Basic documents require students to communicate ideas clearly, concisely, and accurately using appropriate language. More complex documents require students to acquire information from on-line or traditional sources, analyze and evaluate that information, and interpret it before they can prepare the document. These subskills focus on creative thinking, decision making, and problem solving. Preparing the document may require students to simplify the material by illustrating it with charts, graphs, and other symbols to enable the reader to comprehend the material. Students will have an opportunity to develop and apply all of these skills as they work through the applications in *Basic Letter and Memo Writing.*

INSTRUCTIONAL DESIGN

The instructional design provides instructors with the flexibility of using these instructional materials as a basic text in a written communication course or as a supplemental text in a variety of courses that include written communication objectives. The flexible instructional design enables instructors to use the materials in a variety of classroom settings ranging from computer laboratories to traditional classrooms with no electronic equipment. Often instructors use a traditional classroom for instruction and a computer laboratory for outside assignments. Students are encouraged to use either traditional references or electronic reference tools, including spelling verifiers, grammar verifiers, style evaluators, and thesauruses. Technology is presented as a tool to facilitate writing and editing.

The emphasis placed on the mastery of English skills varies considerably depending on the philosophy of the instructor, the background and needs of the students, and the time available for instruction. Basic skills are integrated in both the text and the applications. Two different approaches are used to help students master basic skills in minimum time. The chapter content materials present and review basic writing principles. The design of the applications enable instructors to use a practical, diagnostic approach to ensure that students master basic language arts skills. Documents requiring considerable editing provide the vehicle for diagnosing and reinforcing language arts skills. These documents are keyed to a summary of grammar, punctuation, capitalization, word usage, and number usage guides contained in Appendix B of the student text and Appendix A of this manual. Students use reference tools in these applications just as they would in a business setting.

Although the text is based on sound communication theory, the focus is on practical applications. Scenarios and documents used as illustrations and applications are typical of those found in industry. Students learn the importance of using technology to facilitate communications and the importance of being able to communicate effectively in a global setting. SCANS competencies are incorporated throughout the text and activities. (See pages x and xi in the student text for a correlation chart.)

THE INSTRUCTIONAL PACKAGE

The instructional package consists of four components:

- the text-workbook (0-538-67516-0)
- instructor's manual (0-538-67520-9)
- tests (0-538-67517-9)
- template diskettes (IBM compatible-E0-538-67518-7 and MAC-0-538-67519-5)

STRUCTURE OF THE TEXT-WORKBOOK

The text uses a combined problem-solving and writing strategy, or model approach, for basic types of communication. This approach makes it easy for students to learn the process of planning and writing effective messages and at the same time produce high-quality results very early in the learning experience. Students master basic principles and then apply them to solve easy problems before progressing to more complex business challenges.

Basic Letter and Memo Writing contains ten chapters and four appendices. The first two chapters are designed to introduce and teach basic writing principles. The remaining eight chapters are designed to apply the basic principles to specific writing situations.

Each chapter contains

- Performance goals—competencies that students develop by studying the materials carefully and completing the applications.
- Overview—a preview of the contents of the chapter.
- Chapter content—discussion and illustrations of the topic.
- Connections—a discussion of global and technological issues.
- Internet: The SuperHighway of Communications—information about using the Internet.
- Miscommunications—a look at the lighter side of communications.
- Applications—an opportunity for students to apply what they have learned in the chapter.

The applications in Chapters 1 and 2 vary slightly from those in Chapters 3 through 10. Chapter 1 contains three applications.

- 1A applies the content of the chapter.
- 1B is a self-assessment that students can use to determine if they have mastered the content of the chapter.
- 1C introduces students to Heritage Productions, a case study that continues with applications in every chapter.

Chapter 2 contains four applications.

2A applies the content of the chapter.
2B is an editing and language arts checkpoint.
2C is a self-assessment.
2D is the Heritage Productions case study.

Chapters 3 through 10 contain five applications.

- Application A reviews the basic writing principles.
- Application B is an editing and language arts checkpoint.
- Application C applies the content of the chapter.
- Application D is a self-assessment.
- Application E is the Heritage Productions case study.

Chapter 1—Style, Process, and Product focuses on communication from the perspective of the organization, the employee, and the recipient. It distinguishes between learning the process of writing and developing good results. The chapter illustrates and analyzes writing styles and focuses on adapting style to meet the needs of the reader and the situation. The Connections section reviews the technology used to create, process, and transmit documents. The Internet section distinguishes between intranets and the Internet and introduces the Internet as a tool to facilitate communication.

Chapter 2—Ten Guides for Effective Writing presents and illustrates basic writing principles.

- Guide 1   Plan messages carefully.
- Guide 2   Write for the reader.
- Guide 3   Present ideas positively.
- Guide 4   Write in a clear, readable style.
- Guide 5   Check for completeness.
- Guide 6   Use an efficient, action-oriented style.
- Guide 7   Use concrete language.
- Guide 8   Use effective sentence and paragraph structure.
- Guide 9   Format documents effectively.
- Guide 10 Edit and proofread carefully.

The Connections section focuses on cultural diversity and global competitiveness. The Internet section analyzes the advantages and limitations of E-mail and presents guides for preparing E-mail messages.

Chapter 3—Positive Letters and Memos teaches students how to analyze situations and anticipate the manner in which the reader is likely to react to the message that must be written to solve the situation. The examples used in this chapter illustrate appropriate style and strategy to use for situations in which the reader is likely to be pleased and respond positively or to receive the information in a neutral manner. The strategy recommended is a direct strategy for both positive and neutral messages. The Connections section addresses issues employees experience communicating to culturally diverse customers and fellow employees. The Internet section addresses the security of communications transmitted electronically.

Chapter 4—Negative Letters and Memos focuses on situations in which the reader is likely to be displeased and to respond to the situation in an unfavorable manner. It also addresses mixed-news situations that elicit both favorable and unfavorable reactions. The strategy recommended is an indirect strategy for most negative messages. However, in certain cases, a direct strategy can be used effectively. The Connections section focuses on translation and other challenges that occur when employees deal with international customers. The Internet section focuses on E-mail etiquette.

Chapter 5—Persuasive Letters and Memos focuses on factors that influence persuasion. Ethical issues in persuasion are highlighted. An indirect strategy is recommended for situations in which the reader must be convinced or induced to take action. Brainstorming techniques are presented to help generate creative ideas. The Connections section focuses on techniques to make international messages easier to interpret. The Internet section focuses on using the Internet to locate accurate information efficiently.

Chapter 6—Letter and Memo Reports focuses on messages used for decision making. Managers in industry frequently use letter and memo format when they prepare basic reports. This chapter provides students with experience analyzing, organizing, formatting, and conveying information in an objective, systematic manner. The Connections section emphasizes the differences that may occur in doing business in various cultures. The Internet section presents alternatives for electronic distribution of information.

Chapter 7—Form Letters and Memos explains the need for efficiency as well as effectiveness in preparing documents. The text covers four types of forms—complete forms, variable forms, form paragraphs, and guide forms. The Connections section discusses the technology used to prepare form messages, and the Internet section covers the distribution of form messages electronically.

Chapter 8—Collaborative and Team Writing emphasizes the need to work effectively in teams and presents strategies for team writing. The Connections section presents information about software used for group writing. The Internet section explains the difference between attaching files to E-mail for distribution to team members and Internet software that manages and tracks document revisions made by team members.

Chapter 9—Goodwill and Personal Business Messages focuses on the need to build goodwill and presents strategies for writing thank you, congratulatory, and special occasion messages. Sympathy messages are also discussed. The Connections section focuses on the use of different fonts and clip art for invitations, announcements, and other informal documents.

Chapter 10—Employment Communications address employment both from the perspective of the employer and the employee. Major emphasis is placed on applicant tracking systems and electronic resumes as well as on traditional employment communications. This Chapter may be sequenced at any point after Chapter 5 to prepare students for an effective job search. The Connections section focuses on technology used to automate the employment process. The Internet section focuses on using the Internet as a key component in a job search.

Appendix A—Address Directory is an address file that students use to look up addresses of recipients of application documents, when the addresses are not provided within the text.

Appendix B—Language Arts Checklist is a review of basic language arts guides.

Appendix C—Language Arts Solutions are keyed to the guides in Appendix B so that students can check the appropriate rules for items they missed in Application B.

Appendix D—Evaluation Guide presents students with a checklist to use in evaluating all communications they prepare.

INSTRUCTOR'S MANUAL

This instructor's manual includes the following items:

- Prefatory materials about the instructional package and its usage
- An overview of the text and other components
- A guide for evaluating communications (page 24)
- Teaching suggestions presented on a chapter-by-chapter basis
- Language Arts Checklist (Appendix B in student text)
- Sample solutions for applications (Appendix C in student text)
- Sample solutions for tests
- Transparency masters for each chapter

TEMPLATE DISKETTES

Template diskettes are available for use with this text. The template diskettes contain the editing exercises and can also be used with word processing software for drafting, editing, and revising documents. Students are encouraged to prepare communications at the computer and to use on-line reference tools with all applications.

TEST PACKAGE

The test package is provided in a separate booklet and is available only to instructors. The tests are correlated with the text materials, and the package includes the following:

- Pretest
- Test for each of the 10 chapters
- Posttest

STUDENT FEEDBACK

Providing feedback to students is an integral part of any instructional process. Students should receive feedback on the applications before they attempt the performance evaluations. Feedback can be provided in a variety of ways:

- The instructor can critique students' solutions and make suggestions for improvement.
- Students can critique each other's work.
- Suggested solutions prepared by the instructor or taken from this manual can be given to students for comparison purposes.
- Transparency masters of suggested solutions can be made and projected for students to review. Students' attention can be directed to key points the instructor wishes to emphasize.

GRADING AND EVALUATION

Instructors should inform students of the factors that will be considered in evaluating communications. A suggested scoring guide for evaluating communications is included in this manual and in the text. If this guide is not used, instructors should provide students with the scoring guide that will be used.

STYLE, PROCESS, AND PRODUCT

Chapter 1 is designed to sensitize students to the importance of organizational communications and of developing the ability to communicate effectively. This chapter sets the tone for the strategies that are used in the remaining chapters by having students look at communications from the perspective of the company, the employee, and the recipient of the message. The basic strategy for effective writing is to match the needs of the writer with those of the reader in the context of the situation.

Students need to learn that many alternative modes of communication can be used with differing levels of success. Successful communication is often the result of selecting the proper mode of communication. Making good decisions is a key element in effective communication. The first decision is the selection of the best mode to meet the needs of both the reader and the writer. The situation usually has a significant impact on which mode will be most effective.

Instructors are given the option of having students complete all applications after the entire chapter has been completed or of having students complete each application as soon as the material has been covered in the text. At the appropriate point in the textbook, students are informed that their instructor may direct them to complete a specific application at this point. For example, Application 1A can be completed as soon as the material concerning mode selection on page 2 has been covered.

TYPE AND VOLUME OF COMMUNICATIONS

Students need to understand that a high percentage of all documents are internal documents. Even documents that stay within the company, should be written with care. Many times employees are judged by the quality of the internal documents they produce. The only exposure some employees may have with managers in areas other than their own work units comes from the documents they send to other areas of a company. Sending out quality communications can enhance career opportunities in other areas of the company.

Students also need to understand that preparing communications is costly and time consuming. Therefore, they need to write effective communications in an efficient manner. The primary reason for providing strategies and models is to help students get letters and memos started quickly and effectively.

THE PROCESS OF WRITING

Communications must be approached from both a process and a product orientation. Emphasize to students that writing is a process that can be learned and improved. Students are unlikely to produce perfect letters and memos but they can learn how to write effective letters and memos, and as they gain skill and experience, the product will continue to improve.

STYLE

Style is a key element in writing. Therefore, considerable time and emphasis should be placed on style. Point out that style is a product of the preferences of the writer, the reader, and the situation. Too often writers think of style only from their own perspective. The illustrations are designed to take students from one style extreme to another. Also point out to students that they cannot control or even influence the style of a communication they receive and must answer. They can only react to it. They can use the style to provide clues about the best way to respond to the communication.

CONNECTIONS

The Connections features in each chapter are designed to connect students with developments in two key areas: technology and global communications. These two areas were selected because they are emerging and because they have a tremendous impact on both the quality of communications and the manner in which they are distributed.

This chapter presents an overview of the technology used to prepare and distribute messages. In some institutions, classrooms used for communication classes are equipped with computers and suites of software. In other institutions, classrooms used for communications classes are traditional classrooms, and assignments are prepared in laboratory settings. This section and the applications at the end of the chapter are designed to work effectively with either of these classroom settings.

A key point that must be made to students is that most writers now create their own documents at the computer. The old paradigm of dictating or handwriting documents for a secretary to transcribe is fast disappearing. Students, regardless of career objectives, need to learn how to produce effective documents using computers and appropriate software.

INTERNET—THE SUPERHIGHWAY OF COMMUNICATIONS

The use of the Internet to facilitate communications is growing at an extremely rapid pace; therefore, it is important to teach students how to access information on the Internet and how to judge the quality of that information. Explain that virtually anybody can post information on the Internet and readers have no assurance that the information is accurate. Follow that with a good discussion on the inappropriate uses of the Internet. Many ethical concerns exist, and this section provides a good opportunity to make students aware of the problems as well as the benefits that exist with the Internet.

One concern that can be discussed is employees who spend company time surfing the Internet for reasons that are not essential to business and thereby waste a considerable amount of company time and money. Many companies have had to institute policies about the acceptable use of the Internet.

Students must also understand the difference between the *open* or *public* Internet and the proprietary or company-owned intranets that exist. Security of information is a primary concern to companies; many companies prefer to own their network and to control access to it.

MISCOMMUNICATIONS

This section is included not only to add a little levity to communication problems but also to make students aware of the many miscommunications or bloopers that occur. Encourage students to find examples of miscommunications and to bring them to class. A minute or two spent on these types of situations may help emphasize the communication problems that occur frequently. The local newspaper and the Internet provide great sources of miscommunications that students can locate and bring to class.

NAMING CONVENTIONS FOR TEXT FILES

Teach students how to manage communication files and the importance of naming conventions. Make students aware that what seems like an easy name to remember today may be totally forgotten next week. Emphasize the importance of learning to manage files so that they are easily located. Encourage students to set up directories and to name files in each directory systematically. The names of files in this textbook include the chapter number, the letter representing the application, and the problem number. Students are encouraged to add "rev" to the file name when they save a completed or revised document.

APPLICATIONS

The applications in the textbook are structured to build on previous learnings. The applications in the first two chapters vary slightly from those in the final seven chapters so that a simple-to-complex approach can be used. The following table shows the consistent pattern of applications used to maximize learning.

CHAPTER 1	CHAPTER 2	CHAPTERS 3 THROUGH 10
A Apply Mode Selection Guides	A Apply Guides for Writing	A Review Guides for Writing
	B Editing and Language Arts Checkpoint	B Editing and Language Arts Checkpoint
		C Problem Scenarios
B Self-Assessment	C Self-Assessment	D Self-Assessment
C Heritage Case Study	D Heritage Case Study	E Heritage Case Study

The first application for each chapter always focuses on the presentation or review of basic principles or guides for writing. These basic guides are prerequisite to writing effective messages; therefore, they are given primary attention throughout the text. In Chapter 2, which presents the guides for effective writing, applications can be completed after the material pertaining to each guide is covered or after the entire chapter has been covered. Preferences of instructors vary depending on the class structure and the level and ability of the students. In Chapter 2, students are also introduced to the Editing and Language Arts Checkpoint activity which is designed to assess and reinforce basic language arts and editing skills. This activity is the second application in all of the remaining chapters.

Strategies for writing documents are introduced in Chapter 3. Therefore, beginning in Chapter 3 and continuing through Chapter 10, the third application consists of a series of problem scenarios that require students to write documents following the strategies presented in the chapter. These scenarios are not introduced in the first two chapters because these chapters review basic principles of writing.

The final two applications in all chapters are a self-assessment and a case study. The self-assessment is designed to help students determine if they have mastered the material presented in the chapter. The instructor is provided with additional tests for evaluation purposes. Students do not have access to the tests provided to the instructor for evaluation.

In the case study, students rotate through several "positions" as an assistant manager in different departments of Heritage Productions. Heritage Productions is modeled after an actual company—with significant changes made to names, locations, and proprietary information. The advantage of using this type of continuing case study is that it provides realistic examples for students and provides an opportunity to have students engage in critical thinking and the development of creative ideas that could actually be used in business. The case study involves a global setting and requires students to obtain information from the Internet or traditional library resources if they do not have access to the Internet. A continuing case study gives students the advantage of knowing more and more about the company as they progress through the chapters of the text. They are expected to use the knowledge previously gained or to refer to it if they need to review information presented in previous chapters.

The integration of cultural knowledge with methods for obtaining cultural information is more realistic and valuable than providing a list of dos and taboos for a number of countries. In most cases, those kinds of lists contain stereotypes that are erroneous. A good exercise to make students aware of the fallacies in a "dos and taboos" lists is this: Ask students to complete a dos and taboos list that can be used by citizens of other countries when they visit the United States. It would be extremely difficult to get agreement on what a visitor to the United States should do and avoid doing to be "culturally" sensitive. Knowing the political, economic, or religious situation in a country may be far more important than a list of cultural differences. The Heritage Production case gives students a realistic view of what companies can do to prepare employees who will live in or have extended visits to foreign countries.

Sample solutions are provided in this manual for the applications in each chapter when it is feasible to do so. In some situations, the products students produce will vary so dramatically that a sample solution is not feasible. The solutions presented should be regarded simply as possible guides or illustrations and represent one approach for handling a situation. No solution is perfect. Encourage students to improve the solutions as well as their own work. Obviously, the solutions that students prepare will vary.

SAMPLE SOLUTIONS FOR CHAPTER 1

Select the Best Communication Mode (Page 13)

1. A personal visit would be the best alternative; it would give the individual an opportunity to explain the reasons for the sudden tardiness.

   • E-mail is impersonal; therefore, under the circumstances, it would probably not be acceptable. Because the individual has had a good record and may have a problem, an opportunity to discuss the situation with the individual is much more acceptable.
   • A memo would not be acceptable for the same reasons as E-mail; putting the information in writing may be too strong for an employee with a good performance record when the reasons for the lateness are not known.
   • A telephone call might be acceptable because the situation could be discussed, but it would not be nearly as effective as a personal visit with the individual.

2. A personal visit would probably be the best. A combination might be even better: Follow up the personal visit with an E-mail announcing the award to peers.

   • An E-mail would be acceptable because it conveys the message and can be broadcast to others.
   • A memo would be acceptable because it can become a part of the employee's file.
   • A telephone call is acceptable because you can convey the message—but not as well as in person.

3. A sympathy card would probably be best because the relationship is a business one and you did not know the spouse.

   • A personal letter would be acceptable but it would be difficult to write.
   • A telephone call would be acceptable but may be difficult for the customer.
   • An E-mail would be unacceptable.

4. A fax would be the best alternative because the written document and any drawings can be received instantly.

   • A telephone call would not be appropriate because the information is likely to be technical and lengthy; recording it might result in errors.
   • A letter would not provide the urgent response that this communication requires.
   • An E-mail would have to reproduce standards that are already written. If a file exists containing the standards and the person could easily download that file, E-mail might be acceptable.

5. A letter would be the most appropriate approach.

   • A telephone call would be too personal for this negative situation.
   • An E-mail message may not be secure and may be too impersonal.

APPLICATION 1B

Self-Assessment (Page 15)

1. The decision to use one mode of communication over another is influenced by many factors, such as the

   - anticipated response of the recipient to the way in which information is communicated
   - sensitivity of the situation
   - speed required
   - need for documentation
   - destination (internal or external) of the communication and the accessibility of the recipient
   - costs involved

   For example, many people prefer to transmit sensitive information in a person-to-person setting. Electronic mail, on the other hand, is generally considered informal and impersonal; therefore, it would not be a good alternative for sending sensitive information. Complex information, information needed for future reference, and situations that require documentation should be put in writing. Often, combining modes of communication works better than using a single mode of communication. Most organizations confirm telephone conversations in writing to preserve a record of the information transmitted. A short electronic voice message or written message may alert a recipient to expect detailed information about a particular topic or event.

2. Information that is stored in an electronic database can be accessed by many different employees. Direct access eliminates the need to write many internal documents transmitting information to other employees. The information is also accessible for preparing form documents, which students will learn to do later in the textbook.

3. Style refers to observable behaviors or characteristics. It refers to the manner in which one writes rather than what is written. Formality is a key element of style. Effective communication requires the writer to adapt style to the needs of the reader and to the situation.

4. Application software makes it easy and efficient to create and print documents of high quality. Technology facilitates writing and editing. Documents can also be transmitted electronically, saving time and money.

5. The ability to communicate effectively in writing is one of the skills needed for success in every career. The individual who has developed the ability to communicate effectively in writing has a very marketable skill that will facilitate career growth within an organization and that is transferable to other organizations. Individuals who can communicate effectively are likely to move up in their careers.

CASE STUDY APPLICATION 1C

Heritage Productions (Page 17)

Students' answers may vary widely for these two questions depending on their backgrounds and whether they tried to find information on the topic or simply tried to come up with their own ideas. This situation provides a good opportunity to emphasize to students that when a topic about which they have limited knowledge is going to be discussed in a meeting, they should try to learn more about the topic prior to the meeting so that they can make good contributions. Emphasize to students the importance of using their own initiative and of being a self-starter.

Thoughts about EFL Videos

Check to see that students provide both advantages and disadvantages of using self-paced videos and training materials rather than regular classes. The following list provides examples of advantages and disadvantages.

Advantages

- Self-paced materials are likely to be cheaper than classes with instructors.
- Some people may not be able to attend classes but could work on their own if the time and location were flexible.
- Using videos with business topics would be more realistic than general entertainment-type videos to prepare people for business transactions.

Disadvantages

- An instructor could answer questions and provide better guidance for students.
- Some people are not disciplined or motivated enough to work independently.
- Some people learn better by interacting with others.

Thoughts about Cross-Cultural Videos

Students should agree that it is important for people to understand the culture of countries in which they are doing business because they will be able to deal more effectively with those individuals which will lead to more successful results.

The question relating to Heritage's ability to market these videos effectively is much more difficult. This represents a new venture for Heritage in which Heritage has no experience. Students should think about the similarities between what Heritage currently does and what is proposed. Can Heritage's expertise in marketing in one area transfer to the new venture? Obviously market research will have to be done before investing in this venture. Students may list the kinds of information that would be necessary before a decision can be made.

CHAPTER

TEN GUIDES FOR EFFECTIVE WRITING

BASIC PRINCIPLES

Chapter 2 is a critical chapter, especially for students with average or below average communication skills. The chapter is designed to present and review the basic principles of writing that should be applied in all the chapters that follow. The basic skills focus in this chapter provides instructors with an opportunity to assess the communication skills of their students early in the course and review the skills if needed.

This long chapter is structured into ten segments to give instructors options to present material in the way that best meets the needs of their students. Some instructors prefer to cover all material before doing the applications; others prefer to have students complete applications after each segment of material is presented to give immediate reinforcement. Some instructors provide time for applications to be completed in class; other instructors use the applications for outside assignments. The applications are correlated to each of the ten guides so that instructors can determine which approach works best in a given situation. Each subsequent chapter reviews one of the ten guides presented in Chapter 2. Editing and proofreading skills are reviewed in each of the remaining chapters.

Each of the ten guides contains illustrations to show problems and how the message can be improved significantly by applying the guides. These illustrations are a critical part of the content of Chapter 2. Emphasize to students the importance of analyzing the illustrations carefully to ensure that they understand the guide that is presented.

PROOFREADER'S MARKS

The editing applications require students to use proofreader's marks. The marks are illustrated on page 46 of the student text (and page 17 in this manual). Instructors are encouraged to use proofreader's marks when critiquing papers for students. Students learn a valuable editing skill, and instructors save a considerable amount of time critiquing papers.

GLOBAL CONNECTIONS

Note that the approach used in sensitizing students to the necessity of understanding more about the culture of the individuals with whom they do business is one of learning on a need-to-know basis. Memorizing a list of dos and taboos is not as effective as recognizing the need to gain in-depth knowledge about a particular country if you do business in that country. Again, caution students about the dangers of stereotyping people.

INTERNET—THE SUPER HIGHWAY OF COMMUNICATIONS

This section focuses on E-mail, which is the most common use of the Internet. Remind students of the importance of formatting and editing E-mail messages as well as messages transmitted through regular mail.

Note: All page numbers next to application titles refer to the student text.

APPLICATION 2A

Apply Guides for Effective Writing (Page 49)

Students' answers may vary considerably for these exercises depending on their backgrounds and writing styles. The important things to look for will vary with each guide.

GUIDE 1 PLAN MESSAGES CAREFULLY (PAGES 49–52)

The exercises applying this guide should provide evidence of good planning. The focus should be on having students generate good ideas, use good judgment, and solve problems. The questions are designed to force students to view the situation from the reader's perspective as well as from their own perspective. Answers may vary significantly.

1. a. The main thing you want to accomplish is to assure Ms. Glenn that Turtle Isle Beach Resort can provide her family with an excellent setting for a family vacation so that you will get her business.

   b. Ms. Glenn's objectives are to find a vacation setting that will provide the facilities, services, and environment that will enable her family to have a very enjoyable vacation.

   c. Ms. Glenn is probably a reasonably affluent, older lady who is family oriented. Her request for planned activities and baby-sitting services would indicate that she likes time with the adult children and likes to know that the grandchildren have appropriate activities and good caretakers. The request for beach houses indicates that she probably likes to have the families together in a homelike situation rather than in typical hotel rooms.

   d. The following information should be provided:

   - Brochures showing the beach homes and upscale facilities
   - Schedules of typical activities offered with a notice that activities and schedules may vary from week to week
   - Information about the surrounding area
   - Information about baby-sitting services and other amenities that appeal to young families
   - Information about services you have that are in addition to what she requested

   e. You need to obtain all the information listed in the previous item and have it ready when you begin writing.

   f. The following outline might be a typical approach to writing Ms. Glenn:

   I. Welcome her to bring her family for a memorable vacation
   II. Summarize all the services you offer

   III. Provide cost information

   IV. Refer to the materials that you are enclosing

   V. Assure Ms. Glenn that Turtle Isle Beach Resort will enable her family to have a wonderful, hassle-free vacation that will meet all their family needs.

2. a. You want to provide the owners of Pommery Springs Farms with all the information they requested and to try to secure their business for your employer.

  b. The owners want to receive assurance that Mr. Marks can do a good quality job for them, and they want to know what services are provided and the costs of those services.

  c. The owners are probably affluent people who want privacy and "casual elegance" because the development has a private entrance but they have called it a farm.

  d. You should send them information about the services you offer and the way in which those services are priced. You should also send them information that builds Mr. Marks' credibility, such as a list of customers for whom he has worked or information about developments that they can visit to see his work. You should offer to set up an appointment to visit Pommery Springs Farm and develop a specific, customized proposal for them.

  e. You should collect as much information about Pommery Springs Farm as you can obtain. If the address is provided, drive by and see the property—even take pictures. Obtain the information listed in the previous part of this answer and have it ready.

  f. Outline

    I. Thank them for the request and let them know that you are delighted to provide the information requested.

    II. Provide price information and other information that would make them feel comfortable selecting Mr. Marks as an architect. The owners need to know that Mr. Marks can design the kind of development that meets their needs.

    III. Refer to brochures about Mr. Marks' work, the enclosed cost information, and information about projects he has completed.

    IV. Offer to set up an appointment to visit the site and to develop a customized proposal for Pommery Springs Farm. Assure them that Mr. Marks would be happy to work with them to develop the atmosphere they want to achieve.

3. a. You want to represent your team well and to gain the objective of having the manufacturing plant designated as a no smoking facility.

  b. The human resources manager will be concerned about the impact of the proposed policy on other employees. The manager should be aware of the increasingly negative sentiments against smoking; however, the manager may also feel that dealing with the problem is a hassle. The response may depend on the manager's own feelings about the smoking issue.

  c. You should first of all determine what smoking policies, if any, currently exist and whether those policies are effective. You should also make sure you know how many employees support the policies being proposed. You should locate enough information to justify the request. It would be helpful to reference other companies that have policies similar to the proposed one.

  d. Outline

    I. Introduce your role as team representative and provide information about the team and its working environment.

    II. Request the policy change and provide the reasons why your team would like to see the policy instituted.

    III. Offer to provide additional information if it is needed.

4. a. What objectives do you want to achieve with this memo?

   You want to have 1.5 hours of release time for 12 weeks. You want to be able to participate in the Junior Achievement program and have your company support it.

   b. How do you think your supervisor will respond?

   The supervisor's response will be conditioned by the impact that your missing work will have on your job. Most companies like to see employees participate in community service activities; therefore, your request is likely to be received favorably.

   c. What information must you have?

   You need to have information about the Junior Achievement program if the company is not familiar with it. You also need to provide information about the school and teacher and the specific job you will be doing. You need to provide information about the schedule.

   d. What appeal would be best to use?

   You need to consider what would be the most persuasive way to appeal to your supervisor. Because the company would gain benefits by having employees participate in community service activities, a logical appeal should work well.

   e. Outline

   I. Introduce the idea of working as a Junior Achievement consultant.
   II. Explain why it would be a good thing to do.
   III. Request permission to work as a consultant.
   IV. Close on a warm, friendly note.

GUIDE 2 WRITE FOR THE READER (PAGES 53–54)

1. Please ask the office staff to send the survey out in today's mail.

2. Your check arrived after this month's statement was mailed; therefore, last month's charges were included on the statement.

3. The new product design report you prepared is excellent, and I really like it and will send it to the Design Committee.

4. Please pick up our supplies at the warehouse on your way back from lunch.

5. The Design Committee will consider the new product design at our meeting on Friday. Please read the report I sent you prior to the meeting and be prepared to discuss it. Discussion will begin promptly at 10 A.M.

6. Please ask all managers to ensure that their sales representatives attend the new product training session on October 3 at 9:15 A.M.

7. Please inform our employees that if they want to hear Jane McKee—the attorney from the corporate office—speak, they may go to the meeting.

8. I would appreciate very much your representing me at the meeting.

9. Please fill out the form and bring it to the printer who prints the tags.

10. The stock you bought had good potential, but it also was a high-risk investment.

GUIDE 3 PRESENT IDEAS POSITIVELY (PAGES 55–56)

1. Please schedule the meeting only if you have finished the proposal.

2. Please provide our customer with directions for adjusting our product properly.

3. I plan to be back in the office at noon; please call me after that time.

4. Jim won't be on time for a 9:15 A.M. meeting if he doesn't leave here by 8:30 A.M.

5. Always send a confirmation copy after faxing a bid.

6. Please join me for lunch today if your schedule permits.

7. Please remember to mail the tax form today.

8. As soon as a new mirror arrives, we will replace your scratched mirror.

9. Please call the Help Desk if you need help installing the new software.

10. Please transmit confidential documents only from a workstation that has been cleared for security.

GUIDE 4 WRITE IN A CLEAR, READABLE STYLE (PAGES 57–58)

1. The new on-line real estate service lists four homes that may be of interest to you.

ADDRESS	SQUARE FEET	PRICE
1028 Maple Street	4,200	$258,000
4035 King Street	4,600	$264,500
9374 Sims Alley	4,100	$224,500
9105 Oak Street	4,800	$295,725

2. The supplies you need for the Interior Design I class are
   - a design ruler
   - a furniture template
   - an appliance template
   - graph paper
   - an architectural symbol guide
   - several sharpened pencils
   - an art eraser
   - tracing paper

3. Please notify all employees in your department that they must participate in one of the Excellence in Customer Service—The Competitive Edge seminars. The seminars are scheduled every Friday morning in October and November. Employees must notify Leslie Martin, our training coordinator, as to which session they will attend so that a seat can be reserved and appropriate supplies made available for them.

4. As you requested, I have scheduled you to participate in the Excellence in Customer Service seminar on Friday, September 15.

5. Mr. Marcus cautioned his youngest daughter about her excessive spending, which might lead his neighbors to think he was displaying his wealth.

6. After the discussion ended, Isabelle summarized the views of both those who supported and those who opposed the controversial proposal and promised to provide a summary soon.

7. I resigned as treasurer because of a philosophical disagreement with other leaders in the organization.

8. Will automating the plant result in employee layoffs, or will the major impact be transferring employees to other positions here or in other locations?

9. As you requested last week, I asked our district sales manager to demonstrate our new line of printers at our showroom on March 6. She will have two of our representatives make the presentation at two o'clock for eight guests from your office.

10. The selection process is a complicated one involving

   - screening interviews by recruiters on campus
   - in-company interviews with a manager from the human resources department
   - interviews of candidates who pass the first two screening hurdles by the manager of the department with the position available

GUIDE 5 CHECK FOR COMPLETENESS (PAGES 59–60)

1. You are writing all your employees a memo notifying them of required attendance at a full-day planning retreat at an off-site location.

   Information you must provide:

   - logistical information—date, beginning and ending time, location, and appropriate directions
   - agenda information—what is being discussed and who is presenting the information
   - preparation information—what do employees need to do, if anything, to be prepared for the retreat

   Questions you should anticipate:

   - What is the appropriate attire for the meeting?
   - Who will be there?
   - Is lunch served?
   - How can you be contacted in case of an emergency?
   - How will the work of your unit be handled if all your employees are out?

2. You are writing to sales representatives to inform them that the company will provide an automobile allowance for them to use their own cars and will no longer provide automobiles for them to use.

   Information you must provide:

   - Information about the change, including when and how it will be implemented
   - The amount of the allowance and how it is determined

   Questions you should anticipate:

   - Why is this change being made?
   - Will employees have the option of purchasing the company car and under what terms?

3. You are writing a memo asking your supervisor for permission to purchase a new computer.

   Information you must provide:

   - Justification for purchasing the computer
   - Hardware specifications
   - Software
   - Cost information

   Questions you should anticipate:

   - Is the current system usable or could it be upgraded?
   - Do you have the money available in your budget?
   - What is the payback period (time when the benefits of purchasing the computer exceed the cost of purchasing it)?
   - Is the hardware and software specified compatible with the current equipment and files?

4. You are writing your employees a memo encouraging them to participate in a volunteer work project upgrading homes for the elderly.

Information you should provide:

- Why it is important for companies to support community service
- Name of the organization sponsoring the project
- Logistical information—date, starting time, amount of time expected from volunteers, location
- Appropriate attire and needed tools or supplies, if any

Questions you should anticipate:

- Who else will be working on the project?
- Will employees occur any costs?
- Will employees get work-release time to do the volunteer work?
- How much construction knowledge is needed to do the upgrades?

Indicate the additional information that is necessary in each of the following situations.

5. The Leadership Seminar is scheduled for November 6 at 10:30 A.M. All department managers are expected to participate in the seminar.

Additional information that should have been provided:

- Location
- Ending time
- Information about the program, who is conducting it, and any preparatory work that must be done
- Supplies or materials needed
- Indication of whether lunch is provided

6. Please reserve a room for me at your hotel for June 16 and 17.

Additional information that should have been provided:

- Type of room, such as king or nonsmoking
- Time of arrival and guarantee, if necessary
- Number of people, if any, besides you in the room

7. Will you meet me for lunch at the Market Restaurant on Friday, May 6?

Additional information that should have been provided:

- Time, location, and directions unless person is likely to know the location
- Purpose of lunch if it is other than a social event
- Names of others who are attending, if any

8. You are invited to a reception at my home on Tuesday, March 20 at 6 P.M. honoring Julie McMath for receiving the Innovation Award.

Additional information that should have been provided:

- Address and directions—unless recipient is likely to know both
- Ending time
- Attire—if norms are not generally known (such as business casual)

9. The Planning Retreat scheduled for Friday has been canceled.

Additional information that should have been provided:

- Reason for cancellation
- Information indicating whether it will be rescheduled
- Information indicating whether participants need to do anything about the items that would have been discussed at the retreat.

10. Vice President Jennifer Goldberg from our corporate headquarters will be visiting our plant on October 10.

    Additional information that should have been provided:

    - What is the purpose of her visit?
    - Who will have contact with her?
    - Is preparation for visit necessary? If so, specify what is needed.

GUIDE 6 USE AN EFFICIENT, ACTION-ORIENTED STYLE (PAGES 61–62)

1. Matt thinks that the case may be settled this week.

2. The governor invited Ellen to the reception because she is a member of the board of directors.

3. Please announce that Shelter 2 is available for our use if it rains during the picnic.

4. Natalie shipped a 12-pound box to Columbus, Mississippi.

5. The property owners read and approved the agreement.

6. The furniture was badly scratched during the move. (no change—good use of passive voice)

7. Joseph told the two teams that if they did not cooperate, he would seriously consider not giving them the maximum bonus next quarter.

8. The gift looks nicer in a larger, rectangular box.

9. Did Mary say that John had reverted to unacceptable behavior?

10. Peggy was not only hospitable, she also helped us a lot when we moved to our new home.

GUIDE 7 USE CONCRETE LANGUAGE (PAGES 63–64)

1. Approximately 60 percent of our students work ten hours or more each week in part-time jobs.

2. The flight was six hours long, and it cost $1,000.

3. Bill wants to know if 500 program brochures are available for the mailing that will be sent out on June 10.

4. Please return the questionnaire to me by April 10.

5. Arnie's salary as a surgeon is $50,000 more per year than Dan's salary as a dentist. *Or*

   Arnie earns $250,000 a year as a surgeon; Dan earns $200,000.

6. Susie works until 11 P.M. three nights each week.

7. Pat insists on walking two miles a day.

8. They were two months late paying that $30,000 bill.

9. Please place your book orders by November 6.

10. Does your bank pay 10 percent interest on a $100,000 certificate of deposit?

GUIDE 8 USE EFFECTIVE SENTENCE AND PARAGRAPH STRUCTURE (PAGES 65–66)

1. Do you plan to attend the meeting the president scheduled at two o'clock this afternoon in the auditorium? No agenda was sent out, but I think the new product line will be discussed.

2. On our trips, we prefer to shop for good bargains, to swim in the ocean, and to dress casually.

3. If your payment on your boat is late again, the boat will be repossessed.

4. Please place the magazines near the guest chairs in the reception office.

5. When the estimate was prepared, the price of the monitor was left out.

6. A number of organizations have eliminated layers of management positions in the process of downsizing. *In addition,* the number of individuals seeking management positions is increasing. (Managers with excellent communication skills are in the best position to move up the career ladder in management.) *Therefore,* managers interested in increasing their chances for promotion should work hard to develop good communication skills.

7. Write a three- or four-sentence paragraph explaining why you would prefer to work in a small business rather than a large business. Put parentheses around the topic sentence and underline transitional words.

   Answers will vary widely.

8. List any techniques you used for emphasis in the paragraph you just wrote in No. 7.

   Techniques may include

   * sentence structure
   * mechanical techniques (bold, italics, underline, clip art, etc.)
   * isolation by white space
   * enumerated items

9. Write a paragraph of at least five sentences describing why good computer skills are necessary for most jobs. Place parentheses around the topic sentence and underline transitional words.

   Answers will vary widely.

10. List any techniques you used for emphasis in the paragraph you just wrote.

    Item 8 provides a sample list of things that might be included.

GUIDE 9 FORMAT DOCUMENTS EFFECTIVELY (PAGES 67–68)

1. In a block format letter, all lines begin at the left margin; in a modified-block letter, the date and complimentary close and signature lines are placed near the center.

2. With mixed punctuation, a colon is placed after the salutation and a comma is placed after the complimentary close. Open punctuation has no punctuation after either element.

3. **TO:**   Employees

   FROM: (Student's name)

   DATE: April 23, 1997

   SUBJECT: New Voice Mail System to be Installed

4. Effective format is important for creating a good impression, supporting document content, adding organizational structure, conveying formality, enhancing readability, ensuring consistency, and showing emphasis.

Turkey Creek Farms
294 Crown Lake Drive
Hopkins, SC 29061-2756
(803) 555-0135

Current date

Ms. Cheryl Mayeaux
3948 Devine Street
Columbia, SC 29209-1847

Dear Ms. Mayeaux

We have approved the style manual you provided. As you can see from this letter, block format with open punctuation is now our official letter format. We have also implemented the records management system you proposed.

Your check is enclosed. Thank you for all the work you have done for us.

Sincerely

John A. Lafitte

pr

Enclosure

GUIDE 10 EDIT AND PROOFREAD CAREFULLY

As noted in the student text, review for this guide is provided in Application B of all the remaining chapters.

Write the appropriate symbols used as proofreader's marks to accomplish the edits listed.

a. Delete

b. Transpose

c. Capitalize ≡

d. Move right

e. Use italics ——— *ital*

f. Insert space #

g. Insert an em dash

h. Close space

i. Bold

j. Underline ——— *und*

APPLICATION 2B
Editing and Language Arts Checkpoint (Page 69)

Refer to page 102 of Appendix B for the solution keyed to the language arts guides.

APPLICATION 2C
Self-Assessment (Pages 71–72)

I. 1. After their discussion about the new carpeting for the stadium end zone lounge, Henry sent Ginger a sample of the carpet being used.

2. Always check the academic progress of student athletes and ensure that they are eligible before signing the squad list.

3. Sandy allows you to make tentative appointments provided you remember to get telephone numbers to confirm or cancel the appointment.

4. As indicated in the E-mail announcement, the meeting was rescheduled and will be held on October 10.

5. Why did Jeff place the computer on the end of the table at the back of the boardroom?

6. We will need a lot of shrimp because we are having a big crowd for the reception.

7. Payment for your season pass must arrive before June 15; otherwise, the tickets will be offered in the general ticket sale.

8. Steve Austin, manager of human resources, announced the incentive bonus awards and President Csiszar presented them.

9. The new suite of software includes

   - word processing
   - spreadsheet
   - database
   - graphics
   - clip art
   - project management
   - scheduling
   - Internet access
   - file management
   - accounting

10. Please bring the report to the receptionist by noon on Friday.

II. You have scheduled the quarterly meeting of project managers for October 10. You want each manager to bring a written report summarizing the status of all projects and to be prepared to give a 10-minute update on projections for completion of all projects. List the questions you should ask in planning the memo announcing the meeting and provide short answers for each question.

1. What objectives do you want to accomplish?

   You want to provide managers with all the information needed to prepare for the meeting. You also want to ensure that they have all the logistical information they need.

2. What objectives will your readers have?

   Readers will want to know what they need to do prior to the meeting to prepare for it. They will also want to know all the logistical information about the meeting.

3. What assumptions can you make as you decide what information to send the managers?

   You can probably assume that managers know how to handle their expense accounts for meetings, and they know the appropriate attire for quarterly meetings.

4. Do you have all the information needed to write the memo?

   You know the date, time, purpose, and location of the meeting. You also know that each person has been asked to prepare a report for the meeting. If any participants are from out of town, you may need to get information about hotel and food accommodations and travel.

5. Do you have a mental outline of the memo?

   Use a good news strategy. Begin by providing the most important information first, then supply details, and finally, close on a pleasant note.

III.   A. Inform managers of the meeting and its purpose.

     B. Inform managers of the time, location, who will be participating, and other logistical information.

     C. Request the written report and ask managers to be prepared to make the 10-minute presentation.

     D. Close on a friendly note.

C A S E S T U D Y   APPLICATION 2D

APPLICATION 2D *Heritage Productions, Inc. (Pages 73–74)*

Managers' Brainstorming Session
English as a Foreign Language Videos
(Date is Wednesday of last week)

Potential Markets for EFL Videos

Managers agreed that the EFL videos have significant potential. The three primary market regions considered are Europe, Asia, and South America. The managers decided to select one market and do a pilot test in that market. If the results of the test are good, then they will expand the analysis to the other markets as well.

Regions of Europe

The European market consists of three distinct regions—Northern and Western Europe, Central and Eastern Europe, and Southern Europe. Because these three regions within Europe are quite different and have different advantages and disadvantages, they need to be considered separately.

Europe Selected as First Market Site

After a major discussion of the advantages and disadvantages of each of the alternatives, the managers selected the first site that would be used to test the market. The managers agreed that Europe represented the best opportunity to launch the project.

Advantages. Marketing in Europe offers a number of advantages.

- Heritage's current line of videos in classes is already marketed in Europe.
- Heritage currently has good name recognition in Europe.
- A marketing network is already in place.
- The European market consists of more than 50 countries in which citizens speak about 50 different languages.
- Central and Eastern Europe have few English teachers available so home study video is a good alternative.

Disadvantages. Marketing in Europe also has some disadvantages.

- Extensive competition already exists in Northern and Western Europe.
- British publishers have the bulk of the market for general English training and for school-based programs.
- No one is doing much with English training for business use.
- Market potential in Europe is not as great as it is in Asia, but it is easier to enter.
- Southern Europe (with the exception of Turkey) is not as competitive as Northern and Western Europe.
- Central and Eastern Europe have limited development, but the economy is growing rapidly.
- The laws protecting intellectual property rights are not as strong nor enforced as well in Central and Eastern Europe as in the other two regions of Europe.

Conclusions and Recommendations

The group reached the conclusion that all three sections of the European market have potential for Heritage to market EFL videos successfully. Some entry barriers exist, but the obstacles can be overcome. The most viable and under-served market appears to be Central and Eastern Europe. The group recommended that Heritage target niche markets in Central and Eastern Europe first because of the market size and because the ability to speak English is a prerequisite for high-paying jobs in the region. The group also recommended that Heritage consider partnering with local distributors. This recommendation would need to be investigated very carefully before any decision could be made.

POSITIVE LETTERS AND MEMOS

3

Chapter 3 emphasizes the deliberate use of strategy in writing. Effective planning is a prerequisite for using models strategically. A key element in planning is making sure that the needs of the reader and the situation are taken into consideration before writing the message. Students can be introduced to the concept of adapting to the needs of the reader by discussing scenarios to which they can relate and through which they develop a better understanding of the meaning of empathy. Describe situations in which students might have a positive, a neutral, or a negative reaction. Then talk about designing messages that take those varying responses into consideration. The following examples might be used as a starting point with students.

1. You applied for a loan to purchase a car. Today you received a letter from the bank to which you applied for the loan. Before you open the letter, think about the information it might contain. What do you want to know most? What would please you the most? Think about the response that would please you the least. What other information could the letter contain? How would you react in each of the following situations?

   - The letter indicated your loan was approved.
   - The letter indicated your loan was denied.
   - The letter had nothing to do with your loan; you received a brochure about banking services offered.

2. You interviewed for a $10,000 scholarship. Today you received a letter from the director of the scholarship program. Before you open the letter, think about the information it might contain. What do you want to know most? How would you react if the letter said

   - you won the $10,000 scholarship?
   - you did not win the $10,000 scholarship; but you were a finalist and would receive a $4,000 scholarship?
   - you did not win a scholarship?
   - that information is enclosed about the sponsor of the scholarship for which you are being considered?

Having students react to situations such as these forces them to think about the reader and what a reader might expect when a message is received. Expectations influence the way a message is received, therefore, writers must anticipate the reader's reaction in each situation. Most readers expect the writer to be helpful, fair, considerate, and polite and to make a sincere effort to meet their needs.

USING STRATEGY EFFECTIVELY

Once students learn to think about messages from the perspective of the reader, they will move logically toward designing messages that meet the needs of the reader. Writing strategies need to be introduced very carefully. Strategy evolves from an analysis of the reader's needs. The emphasis is on determining how to meet the needs of the reader in a particular situation. A subtle but important difference exists between following a model and using a strategy designed to meet the reader's needs. A model is a general planning tool that determines the order of information. A strategy considers not only the order of information but also how that information can be tailored to the specific needs of the reader. A strategy is more specific than a model.

Both model and strategy approaches simplify letter and memo writing—particularly for students with little experience in writing. The real value of a model is that it enables the writer to determine the best order for presenting information and to get started quickly. Models are really organizational techniques. However, the use of models can lead to stereotyped messages unless care is taken to design each message to meet the specific needs of the reader. Models should be used to facilitate careful planning—not to replace careful planning. Therefore, students need to understand that the model approach is best utilized when it is coupled with the problem-solving approach described in Chapter 2, Guide 1 and reviewed in this chapter. Using a problem-solving strategy is the best way to prevent messages from becoming stereotyped.

STRATEGY FOR GOOD-NEWS MESSAGES

The strategy recommended for good-news messages is a direct, straightforward approach to writing. Presenting good news as early as possible makes a great first impression and sets the tone for the entire message. Setting a positive tone is highly desirable. Encourage students to analyze the illustration on page 78 very carefully to understand how the strategy is applied. The illustration also presents a good opportunity to show students how the emphasis techniques they learned in Chapter 2, Guide 8, on page 35 can be applied effectively.

STRATEGY FOR NEUTRAL MESSAGES

Again, a good way to start students thinking about a strategy for writing neutral messages is to use a scenario to which students can relate. The following examples might be a good way to get started.

1. You are listening to a classmate talk at length about something that you think is boring and unimportant. How carefully do you listen? Are you likely to tune the person out and think about other things?

2. You are reading a new book that has a lot of introductory detail that is of limited interest to you. How likely are you to put the book aside and do something else?

Point out to students that the way to get people's attention and hold it is to start with the most important information and to present details in as concise a manner as possible. Avoid the temptation to present too much detail.

Remind students that the emphasis techniques apply to neutral messages as well as to good-news messages. Logical thinking makes it clear that the most important information should be presented in the position that gets the most emphasis and less important information should be placed in less emphatic positions. Encourage students to analyze the illustration on page 80 to see how the strategy is applied.

DOCUMENT FORMAT

You can use the two illustrations in this chapter to emphasize the importance of using appropriate letter and memo format. When you talk about first impressions, remind students that readers see the format before they read a document. The first impression comes from the document's appearance.

Because students begin to write letters and memos in this chapter, this is a good time to review the formatting guides presented in Chapter 2, Guide 9, on pages 41–43. In addition to the mechanics of formatting, it is important to discuss image, corporate identity, and standardization issues. Students need to understand that format styles vary from company to company. However, companies that are image conscious often provide employees with standardized guides for formatting all communications produced within the company.

Several points about standardization of document format should be made:

- Format impacts the image of a document and an organization. An older, more conservative, and traditional organization may opt to use modified block style as its standard letter format because it presents a more conservative image. An organization that wishes to project a more modern, progressive image may opt to use block style as its standard letter format.
- Standardizing the format helps an organization present a consistent image—customers or clients always get the same visual impression regardless of who originates the document.
- Formats influence productivity. Once a style has been standardized, it can be stored in the word processing software and used to prepare documents efficiently.

The standardized format for all illustrations in this textbook is block style with open punctuation. The memo heading illustrated on page 80 of this chapter is the standardized memo format for this textbook. You may want to suggest that each student select a standard format for all communications. Require students to justify the format selected. Another alternative is to have students determine a standardized format for the entire class.

DOCUMENT NAMING CONVENTIONS

In addition to standardizing format, students should be encouraged to think about standardizing the conventions used to name document files. Review the naming conventions discussed on page 12 of Chapter 1. An alternative is to standardize naming conventions.

EVALUATING COMMUNICATIONS

One version of a scoring guide for evaluating documents that the students prepare is contained in Appendix D of the student textbook and also on the following page. Instructors are encouraged to provide students with a copy of the guide that will be used to evaluate the students' work if the guide differs from the one presented in this text.

Major emphasis should be placed on having students evaluate their own work. A good way to start is to have a team of students work together to critique the documents written by each member of the group. At this point, discussing general guides for evaluating communications would be helpful to students. The list of questions on page 24 are useful as self-evaluation tools rather than as a scoring guide.

SAMPLE SOLUTIONS

The solutions presented in the instructor's manual illustrate one approach for solving the problems contained in the text. Student solutions may vary widely. The solutions provided in this manual or solutions prepared by the instructor can be used to provide feedback to students. They can be handed out or projected for students to compare to the solutions they prepared.

 # Assess Each Communication

1 **Does the communication accomplish its objective?**

A message is effective if it meet the needs of both the reader and the writer and is appropriate for the situation.

2 **Is the communication objective and logical?**

A communication should be factual, and decisions should be based on sound, logical reasons. The message should present adequate information to support the decisions made.

3 **Is the tone positive and confident?**

The message should convey the impression that the writer is knowledgeable and credible. It should build goodwill and focus on what can be done rather than on what cannot be done.

4 **Is the communication the right length?**

Only those ideas essential to conveying the message completely and effectively and to ensuring courtesy and building goodwill should be included. Ideas should be conveyed in a concise, but courteous manner.

5 **Is the message clear and easy to understand?**

A message is clear if the reader understands the message without having to reread any part of it. Sentences and paragraphs are reasonably short, and vocabulary is appropriate. Tables, illustrations, and graphic aids are used when appropriate to simplify content.

6 **Is the message coherent?**

The words, sentences, and paragraphs should be sequenced logically and flow smoothly. They should fit together to convey a message. Appropriate transitional words should be used to link ideas.

7 **Are important ideas emphasized?**

The reader should be able to discern which ideas the writer considers more important and which are less important than others.

8 **Does the communication have unity?**

The message should have a sense of wholeness; that is, the reader should be able to discern a beginning, middle, and end. All ideas in a paragraph should be related to one topic.

9 **Is the writing style effective?**

The message should be interesting and free of clichés, platitudes, and outdated expressions. It should convey a considerate, pleasant, and helpful tone that is appropriate for the situation.

10 **Does the message create a good image?**

The format and physical appearance should support the message, be consistent, and create a favorable impression.

Review Guide 1: Plan Messages Carefully (Page 83)

APPLICATION 3A

1. Letter to Ms. Wong

   a. Your objective is to convey the message that the credit limit will be extended because Ms. Wong managed her account effectively. You want her to be a satisfied customer who will buy her furniture from your company.

   b. Ms. Wong wants to know that she has additional credit to buy the furniture she desires. She wants to continue doing business with your company.

   c. She is the type of customer you want to keep—she buys expensive furniture and pays her bills in a timely manner.

   d. You should present the good news—that her request has been granted—first to set a positive tone for the entire letter.

      I. Grant the credit.
     II. Explain the terms and conditions.
    III. Offer to be of service and indicate your pleasure to work with her.

2. Memo to employees

   a. You want the offices to be ready for the painters. You also want to ensure that the operation of the office continues smoothly and that sensitive materials are secured.

   b. Employees want to know what their options are and what is expected of them while the work is being done.

   c. Employees will probably like the idea of having their work environment improved but may consider having to clean up and move out of their offices a hassle. Therefore, the best strategy is to treat the situation as good news and start with the positive idea of improving the office. Then explain the details and end on a positive note. This strategy is best because it conveys a positive message to employees and de-emphasizes the hassle by burying the instructions in the middle of the message.

   d.   I. Announce that the painting will be done and the schedule.
     II. Indicate the options available and the security procedures.
    III. Close with the pleasant prospects of working in an improved environment.

3. Letter to Mr. Mendoza

   a. You would like Mr. Mendoza to conduct seminars at the same rate and including the same content for two additional groups of employees.

   b. Mr. Mendoza would like additional business.

   c. You know that his seminars met your needs and that he accepted the rate of pay you offered. He will probably be pleased to have additional business.

   d. Present the good news that his seminars were successful and that additional employees need the training. The good news will set the tone for the entire message.

   e.   I. Explain the need for additional seminars.
     II. Present the logistical and compensation information.
    III. End with a positive comment about the training and looking forward to working with Mr. Mendoza again.

APPLICATION 3B
Editing and Language Arts Checkpoint (Page 85)

Refer to page 104 of Appendix B for the solution keyed to the language arts guides.

APPLICATION 3C
Writing Positive and Neutral Messages (Pages 86–87)

Sample solutions for the nine documents are shown on pages 29–33.
Note that the scenarios expose students to the following industries:

- Retail
- Shipping
- Manufacturing
- Transportation
- Tourism
- Medical/health
- Education
- Telecommunications
- Business services

APPLICATION 3D
Self-Assessment (Pages 88–89)

1. Short Answer

   a. A direct strategy that involves presenting the most important information first, then the less important details, and closing on a positive, helpful note is the most appropriate strategy to use for a routine message. This strategy works because it is logical and places emphasis on the most important information and sets a positive tone for the entire message.

   b. A direct, straightforward strategy is best for good-news messages because it has both logical and psychological advantages. The strategy involves presenting the good news, then the details, then closing on a positive note. Since people like to hear good news, the logical approach is to tell them the good news first. The psychological advantage is that good news makes the reader comfortable with the message; thereby creating a good first impression and setting the tone for the message. The less important details receive less emphasis when they are placed in the middle of the communication.

   c. Planning a message carefully and designing it to meet the needs of the specific reader and the situation prevent the message from being stereotyped.

   d. The good news strategy uses position to create emphasis. The most emphatic positions are the opening and closing. Good news is presented in these positions. The least emphatic position is the middle. Routine information is presented in the middle position.

   e. Six steps are involved in planning a good-news message.

      I. Determine your objectives and try to anticipate the objectives of the reader.
      II. Analyze the reader so that you can adapt your message to the reader's needs. Use information you know about the reader to determine the appropriate vocabulary level, the amount of detail to provide, and to personalize the message.

    III. Make all decisions prior to writing so that you can determine the best strategy to use in presenting the information.

    IV. Collect all the information needed for the message so that it can be organized and communicated effectively.

    V. Develop a writing plan—either a written outline or at least a mental outline.

    VI. Implement the plan by writing the message.

2. Plan the letter to Dr. Evelyn Jervey

    a. You want Dr. Jervey to meet with your supervisors so that they can be comfortable with the process she uses and to get the information you need to make a final decision on her proposal.

    b. Dr. Jervey submitted a proposal so obviously she would like to have the consulting job.

    c. Dr. Jervey is an experienced consultant who understands how decisions to hire consultants are made. She should be pleased with the opportunity to visit your company to present information to your key supervisors.

    d. The first thing you should tell Dr. Jervey is that you are very interested in the proposal she submitted and would like to invite her to visit your company. This good news sets a positive tone for the entire message.

    e.   I. Tell her the good news that you are interested in her proposal.
       II. Invite her to come to your company to meet with your supervisors.
       III. Present the logistical details.
       IV. End on a positive note indicating that you are looking forward to visiting with her.

3. See page 33 for a sample letter to Dr. Jervey.

C A S E   S T U D Y   APPLICATION 3E

Heritage Productions (Page 90)

This exercise has a much broader objective than the other exercises. It is designed to get students more involved in one company on an ongoing basis. Several points need to be made with students.

- Always do your best regardless of what you are asked to do. Good performance opens up opportunities to do more challenging things.
- Learning how to find information is a very important career skill. On-line sources of information add a new dimension to library resources that are now available.
- A lot of information is available but much of it may not be worthwhile. The ability to select the appropriate information from the mass that is available is another important career skill.
- Learn to organize information effectively and communicate it concisely.

By design, students are given limited instructions to encourage them to be creative and to learn to find the information they need. The last question will set them up for future exercises that use different types of information to make projections when direct sources are not available.

1. Students are likely to locate a large amount of information about English as a foreign or second language. Much of the information is about programs available to teach English as a foreign language in specific countries. Some of the material focuses on aids for teachers specializing in teaching English as a foreign language. A lesser amount of the material talks about English as the universal language for conducting business. Information is also available on tests of English language proficiency.

2. The primary providers of information on the Internet are universities and foreign language institutes. Publishers also provide some information about materials available.

3. Students will find less information about training videos than they found about ESL programs in general. An occasional film or video program may be located. The videos are likely to be tapes of programs rather than specially designed training videos.

4. Students are likely to find home pages for English as a second language that have links to numerous other sources. These types of references would be good ones to point out to Mr. Kiely. The specific references probably will vary dramatically among students.

5. Students are not likely to find information about EFL/ESL in Central or Eastern European countries. Very little information on the topic is available; what is available is difficult to access.

6. See sample letter on page 34.

VanHuss Industries, Inc.

TO: All Employees

FROM: Student's Name

DATE: Current Date

SUBJECT: Work Environment Improvement

You will be pleased to know that when we return to work next Monday all the offices in our department will be freshly painted. The painters are scheduled to begin work at noon on Friday.

To prepare for the painters, we all need to clear the desk and furniture tops in our work areas before noon next Friday. Please ensure the security of company files and documents while outsiders are working in the office area by locking file cabinets and logging off the computer network. On Friday afternoon, you may work in any of the following locations:

- Your home
- The departmental conference room
- The employee lounge
- The customer demonstration room

Next week we will all enjoy a pleasant, much improved working environment.

ms

Application 3C–2

South Side Furniture Gallery
4857 Crestwood Road ■ Des Moines, IA 50310-5485 ■ (515) 555-0137

Current date

Ms. Poh-Lin Wong
574 Fifth Avenue
Des Moines, IA 50309-1864

Dear Ms. Wong

Your new $5,000 credit limit is now available to purchase the additional dining room and bedroom furniture you desire. You have maintained your account in an exemplary manner, and we are happy to accommodate your request to increase your credit limit from $1,000 to $5,000.

The same terms and conditions of your current credit account apply. All you need do is select your new furniture and sign the sales agreement. Our sales representative will take care of all of the details for you.

Ms. Wong, we hope you enjoy your new furniture. We appreciate your business and look forward to working with you for many years to come.

Sincerely

Student's name
Credit Manager

ms

Application 3C–1

VanHuss Industries, Inc.

TO: Brad Cubbage, Shipping Manager

FROM: Student's Name

DATE: Current Date

SUBJECT: Shipping Containers

The Kerry Container Company is my recommendation for a new supplier for containers to use in shipping the gas grills we manufacture. Several alternatives were evaluated, but the Kerry product best meets our needs.

The Kerry container is six pounds heavier than our current container and meets all of the specifications agreed upon by the Shipping Department. The cost is approximately the same, but the added container weight will have a slight impact on shipping costs. However, savings resulting from the lower damage rate will more than offset the additional shipping cost. As you will note from the attached cost analysis and technical specifications, the Kerry product offers the protection we need at a reasonable cost.

If the Kerry Container Company is approved as our new supplier, we should meet with their representatives as soon as possible to work out procedures for maintaining inventory, quality control, and billing.

ms

Attachments

Application 3C–4

VanHuss Industries, Inc.
4820 Forrest Drive ■ Albany, NY 12205-6927
(518) 555-0124

Current date

Mr. Roberto Mendoza
5938 Blossom Road
Rochester, NY 14610-4298

Dear Mr. Mendoza

The seminars on financial planning that you conducted for our employees were very successful, and we continue to get good feedback on them. We have identified two additional groups of employees who would benefit from having this training, and we hope that you will be able to conduct two more seminars for us.

We would again offer you $1,500 per day for this training. The seminars can be scheduled at your convenience during the next month or two.

We look forward, Mr. Mendoza, to having you work with our employees again. We know that they will benefit from the excellent training you provide. Please call me by next Friday so we can confirm dates for the seminars.

Sincerely

Student's Name

ms

Application 3C–3

VanHuss Industries, Inc.
9081 Packer Drive ▪ Green Bay, WI 54304-2536
(414) 555-0150

Current date

Mr. William Kerry
Kerry Container Company
P.O. Box 3857
Milwaukee, WI 53201-3857

Dear Mr. Kerry

Kerry Container Company has been selected as the new supplier for containers used to ship the gas grills we manufacture. Our Shipping Manager, Brad Cubbage, approved the specifications and price quotations that you supplied.

Our Shipping Team would like to meet with you or your representatives on Tuesday, *insert date*, at 2:30 p.m. The purpose of the meeting would be to work out appropriate procedures for inventory management, quality control, and billing. Please let us know if this date and time is acceptable.

We look forward to a long and mutually beneficial relationship with Kerry Container Company.

Sincerely

Student's Name

ms

Application 3C–5

Holiday Air, Inc.

P.O. Box 6958
Columbia, SC 29201-6958
(803) 555-0152

Current date

Ms. Ursula Pharr
MBA Managing Director
College of Business
Central University
Irmo, SC 29063-8447

Dear Ms. Pharr

Holiday Air is proud to be a sponsor of the Central University MBA Case Competition team. We are delighted to provide the six members of your team with round-trip tickets to the three cities hosting the competition.

Please provide me with the names, addresses, and telephone numbers of the six team members. We will also need the preferred flight dates and schedules for all three trips. As soon as we receive this information from you, one of our reservations agents will call you to finalize the arrangements.

We wish your team success in the competitions, and we look forward to having them aboard Holiday Air.

Sincerely

Student's Name
Marketing Manager

ms

Application 3C–6

Central University MBA

TO: MBA Case Competition Team

FROM: Student's Name

DATE: Current Date

SUBJECT: Holiday Air Sponsorship

Great News! Holiday Air has agreed to sponsor our MBA Case Competition Team. As sponsor, Holiday Air will provide free tickets for each of you to travel to the three host cities in which you compete.

I am providing Holiday Air with your names, addresses, and telephone numbers as well as our preferred flight dates and schedules for all three trips. You will receive additional information as soon as the travel plans have been finalized.

Mr. Bruce Rosenfield, Marketing Manager of Holiday Air, is the person responsible for sponsoring us. I am sure he would appreciate receiving a thank you note from each of you.

ms

Application 3C—7

Montreal Bound

TO: MBA Case Competition Team

FROM: Student's Name

DATE: Current Date

SUBJECT: Montreal—A Great Place to Visit

Our competition schedule provides ample time to enjoy the charm of Montreal. Maps of downtown Montreal and Old Montreal are attached. We will be staying near Olympic Park, which is known for its concerts, shows, and sporting events. A list of restaurants in the Olympic Park area and the Old Montreal area is also attached.

In downtown Montreal, travel is easy on the Metro. You will also find a whole underground city with malls, museums, shops, and eateries. Since the weather outside will be quite chilly, the underground will be a welcome way to get around the town.

To experience Old Montreal in a delightful way, plan to take the Calèches (horse-drawn sight-seeing buggies) for a tour of the historic area. The Old Port has marvelous cafes and shops.

The Internet provided a wealth of information about Montreal, and I have put together a travel packet for the team. The travel packet contains information about the following points of interest:

- The Underground City
- Old Saint-Sulpice Seminary and Clock
- Dorchester Square
- Old Montreal and the Old Port
- The Sailor's Church
- The Cathedral-Basilica Mary Queen of the World and Saint James the Greater
- The Botanical Garden
- The Olympic Park

Application 3C—8

VanHuss Industries, Inc.
292 Crown Lake Drive ■ Hopkins, SC 29061-4736
(803) 555-0181

Current date

Dr. Evelyn Jervey
Jervey and Associates
P.O. Box 2847
Hopkins, SC 29061-2847

Dear Dr. Jervey

Your proposal to evaluate our entire customer service operation is of great interest to us, and we would like to explore it further. Our key supervisors would like to know more about the processes that you propose to use in your evaluation.

We invite you to meet with our key supervisors either on Tuesday or Thursday, *Insert dates*, at 9:30 in the morning. The meeting should take approximately an hour. Please let me know if either of these times fit in your schedule.

We look forward to meeting with you and hope to be able to work with you on improving our customer service operation.

Sincerely

Student's Name
Manager of Customer Service

ms

Application 3D–3

Midlands Medical Center
375 Lincoln Street ■ Durham, NC 27710-0987
(919) 555-0120

Fred C. Stands, MD

Current date

Mr. J. T. Teng
4856 College Avenue
Chapel Hill, NC 27515-2948

Dear Mr. Teng

The results of your laboratory tests were negative.

Mr. Teng, it is really important that you follow both the diet and the exercise program that we prescribed for you. You should schedule your follow-up visit in six weeks. Of course, if you experience any problems prior to that time, you should contact me immediately.

To schedule your next appointment, or if you have any questions about either the prescribed diet or exercise program, please call our office assistant at the number shown above.

Sincerely

Fred C. Stands, MD

ms

Application 3C–9

Heritage Productions, Inc.

Heritage Productions

TO: Mr. Gary Kiely

FROM: Student's Name

DATE: Current Date

SUBJECT: EFL Resources

Surfing on the Internet produced a tremendous number of EFL resources. Much of the information I located on the Internet related to programs in various countries that are available to teach English as a foreign language. Some of the material focused on aids for teachers specializing in teaching English as a foreign language. A few resources related to using English as the universal language for conducting business. I also located information about tests of English language proficiency that are available.

The bulk of the information about English as a second language came from universities and foreign language institutes that offer English training. A few resources were provided by publishers. Very little of the information related specifically to videos designed for training purposes. The references generally related to tapes of news or entertainment programs that were used so that students could hear English spoken.

Using EFL and ESL as keywords produced much of the information located. The English as a Second Language Home Page and the English as a Foreign Language Home Page on the World Wide Web are excellent places to get a feel for the various types of information available on the Internet. Sample material printed from those sites is attached.

Specific information on EFL/ESL in Central or European countries is not readily available. I will continue to search for information specifically related to the countries we are considering as target markets and report back to you by next Wednesday.

ms

Attachment

Application 3E–6

NEGATIVE LETTERS AND MEMOS

4

Chapter 4 reinforces the emphasis on the deliberate use of strategy in writing that was taught in previous chapters. Negative letters are particularly difficult for students to write. Point out to students that bad-news letters are difficult even for experienced writers because of the concern for offending the reader. Students need to understand that decisions may seem to be clear-cut on the surface, but often decisions are reversed because companies will take a loss on a particular situation rather than risk losing a good customer. Conceptual skill—the ability to see the big picture—is necessary for making effective decisions about situations that will be considered bad news by the reader.

PLAN EFFECTIVELY

Encourage students to pay particular attention to the planning process. The key questions listed in the margin on page 92 of Chapter 4 should be used as the basis for class discussion. The need to check out facts before writing bad-news letters cannot be overemphasized. The damage done in these types of situations often is impossible to reverse.

Forcing students to use empathy and to analyze the severity and sensitivity of issues helps them develop good interpersonal skills, which are critical to success in their careers. Point out to students that the more sensitive an issue, the more important it is to make wise decisions about the message to be conveyed and the medium used to convey that message. The six questions presented on pages 92–93 are designed to reinforce the decision-making abilities that were presented in Chapter 1. Judgment is needed in many of the situations. Class discussion should be encouraged. Students often will make different decisions. Requiring them to justify their decisions and to speculate on the reaction of the reader and then to compare their justifications with those of their peers may help them view the situation from a different perspective. Giving students experience in making judgments when situations are not clear-cut is very valuable.

STRATEGY FOR BAD-NEWS MESSAGES

The primary strategy recommended for bad-news messages is an indirect approach to writing that uses a buffer to provide an opportunity to explain the reasons for a decision before presenting the bad news. Most students will not have had any experience using a buffer. They need to understand that a buffer is not just a delay tactic, it is a sincere attempt to make sure that the reader understands that the decision was made in a fair and equitable manner. Emphasize that a good buffer

- is neutral
- is relatively short
- leads logically to the reasons for a decision
- does not mislead the reader in any way

Remind students that stereotyped closings usually do not work with negative letters. A critical part of the planning is determining an effective way to end the message. A neutral or goodwill gesture to end a letter leaves a better impression than a negative statement.

Encourage students to analyze the illustration on page 93 very carefully to understand how the strategy is applied. The illustration also presents a good opportunity to show students how the emphasis techniques they learned in Chapter 2 can be reversed to de-emphasize negative information.

STRATEGY FOR MIXED-NEWS MESSAGES

Remind students that, by definition, a mixed message contains both good and bad news. Although it is nice to have something good to include, students need to remember that the bad news must be dealt with effectively. A direct strategy is appropriate for the good news, but it is important to present the reasons for the bad news clearly and tactfully in a way that leads logically to the decision made. Because bad news follows the good news, toning down the presentation of good news is usually a wise approach.

Encourage students to analyze the illustration on page 100 to see how the strategy is applied.

ALTERNATIVE STRATEGIES FOR NEGATIVE MESSAGES

The use of indirect strategy for negative letters is not universally recommended. Indirect strategy applied appropriately can be very effective. At the same time, a direct strategy can also be very effective, particularly for product or service-related problems.

Teaching students both the direct and indirect strategies and appropriate situations for using each strategy emphasizes the importance of carefully analyzing the situation and the expected reaction of the reader. Make sure that students understand that even though a direct strategy works effectively for claims letters, the problem still must be handled in a very sensitive manner.

The tendency of students is to use too much force or make statements that are stronger than necessary. Point out to students that additional force can be used in a follow-up message if the first message did not produce the desired result. The reverse is not true, however. If a message is too strong and offends the reader, the damage cannot be undone.

A factual, unemotional approach usually is most effective when reporting problems to an organization. The illustration on page 101 provides an example of a factual, unemotional tone. At the same time, the message is very direct. Note in the first paragraph that the emphasis is on making sure the reader understands the problem. It does not accuse, sermonize, or berate the reader for the problem.

GLOBAL CONNECTIONS

Emphasize to students that global is local. Too often students think they are in their own communities and are not affected by global situations. Use very mundane situations to emphasize how global events affect everybody—even small, rural communities. For example, hair stylists are often asked to cut a person's hair in the same style worn by a celebrity in another country. Many imported products use metric measurements rather than the measuring standards Americans are accustomed to using. Fax and E-mail make it very easy to communicate to individuals in different countries; therefore, more employees than ever before are involved in communicating to individuals in other regions of the world. This exercise presents a good opportunity to talk about the reasons for using a fax cover sheet and the type of information to include on the cover sheet.

Using the sections on global communications and technology connections for class discussion helps to sensitize students to cultural differences. Encourage students to surf the Internet to find information about other cultures. Team projects are useful. A class can be divided into several teams and each team can select a different country with which to "do business." Have teams compare the cultural differences in the various countries researched.

SAMPLE SOLUTIONS

The solutions presented in the instructor's manual illustrate one approach for solving the problems contained in the text. Student solutions may vary widely. The solutions provided in this manual or solutions prepared by the instructor can be used to provide feedback to students. Solutions can be handed out or projected for students to compare to the solutions they prepared.

Review Guide 2: Write for the Reader (Page 105)

1. Please meet with your employees and ask that they read the new procedures very carefully. Please explain to your employees the importance of attending the meeting that will explain how the procedures are to be implemented.

2. Please modify your project so that it conforms to the directions provided and resubmit it as quickly as possible.

3. All department heads should ensure that their expenditures are within their budgets.

4. Thank you for the excellent work you did to ensure that your project was successful.

5. Please ask our office staff to find an appropriate room for the meeting and request that the room be set up properly.

Editing and Language Arts Checkpoint (Page 106)

Refer to page 105 of Appendix B for the solution keyed to the language arts guides.

Writing Negative and Mixed-News Messages (Pages 107–110)

APPLICATION 4C

Sample solutions for the seven documents requested in exercises 2, 4, 6, 7, 8, 9, and 10 are on pages 41–44. Note that the scenarios expose students to the following industries:

- Retail
- Shipping
- Manufacturing
- Transportation
- Tourism
- Real estate

- Education
- Technology/telecommunications
- Business services

For the first three documents (exercises 1, 3, and 5) students are lead through a step-by-step planning process to give them experience applying each of the writing strategies presented in the chapter. Then students are asked to plan and write additional documents independently.

1. Planning

    a. The reader is likely to be disappointed, but the situation is not likely to be sensitive because the reader is asking for something that would be a gift.

    b. You would like to build goodwill with the university even though you cannot grant the current request.

    c. A sentence implying that you gave the situation every possible consideration.

    d. You can't afford to give free tickets during your peak demand time, and you have even blocked out your most valuable customers from using free tickets during this time.

    e. You can offer tickets at a nonpeak time.

    f. Wish the team success with their competition.

2. See sample letter for 4C-2 on page 41.

3. Planning

    a. The reader will be pleased that you are keeping part of the order and disappointed that you are canceling the rest of the order and returning the jacket.

    b. Starting with the good news will set a positive tone for the letter, but because this is a service problem, a factual approach would also be appropriate.

    c. You ordered the items for a special cruise, and your cruise will depart before the items are scheduled to arrive.

    d. You can close with stating your appreciation for a prompt refund.

4. See sample letter for 4C-4 on page 41.

5. Planning

    a. It would be appropriate to use a direct approach because this letter is about a product claim from a customer.

    b. The reader is likely to be displeased that you have a problem with the software, but should be eager to solve the problem and keep the customer satisfied.

    c. Explain the problem in a factual way with adequate information to solve the problem.

    Describe your request for action providing adequate justification.
    Close on an optimistic note.

6–10. See pages 42–44 for sample letters.

APPLICATION 4D

Self-Assessment (Page 111)

1. Short Answer

   a. The most appropriate strategy for a message that conveys negative information is an indirect approach because it enables the writer to begin on a neutral note and present the reasons for the bad news before it is disclosed.

   b. A good buffer is a concise, neutral statement that leads into the reasons for a negative decision. A good buffer deals with the subject and does not mislead the reader into thinking that positive information follows. It cushions the blow of negative news.

   c. A direct approach is most appropriate for a claims situation that involves problems with products or service. The situation is not as sensitive because the reader wants to resolve the problems and maintain the customer.

   d. The severity and the sensitivity of the situation are the factors that most influence the choice of media. Decisions that have a very negative impact on the reader and that are likely to anger the reader may need to be conveyed in person rather than in written form. Information that is not sensitive might be appropriately conveyed in the most convenient method, such as E-mail.

   e. Negative information can be de-emphasized by reversing the emphasis techniques learned earlier. Examples include:

   - Avoid using attributes such as bold, underscoring, and all capitals.
   - Limit the amount of space devoted to the negative information.
   - Avoid isolating the negative information in one-line paragraphs or in areas with excessive white space that draw attention to the item.
   - Use complex and compound sentences, which are less emphatic than simple, direct sentences. Place negative ideas in the dependent clause of complex sentences to receive less emphasis.
   - Use general language and passive voice because they are less emphatic than specific language and active voice.
   - Bury negative ideas in the middle paragraphs of a message and in the middle sentences of a paragraph to de-emphasize them.

2. See sample letter 4D-2 on page 44.

C A S E   S T U D Y   APPLICATION 4E

Heritage Productions (Page 112)

Students should have accumulated a reasonable amount of information about Heritage Productions at this time. This exercise forces them to use information provided to them about Heritage products in Chapters 1 and 2. Ask students to describe Heritage's key products and target markets before discussing this assignment.

1. In the application, Mr. Kiely makes it clear that he does not want to schedule the trip at this time unless compelling business reasons make it urgent to do so. Nothing in the information produced could be considered as compelling reasons to go immediately; therefore, the invitation should be declined.

2. The good news is that the information was available and that the trip is not urgent. The bad news is that Stonehedge does not offer good business opportunities that Heritage needs to pursue at the present time.

3. The letter is a bad-news situation because you are declining an invitation. However, the situation is not very sensitive. A goodwill close can be presented by holding out the offer to visit in the future and by inviting Ms. Addison to visit your organization.

   Note that the fax cover sheet could have been prepared using a template from word processing software or could have been designed by the student. Check to see that it includes the following information as a minimum:

   Recipient's name, fax number, and telephone number
   Sender's name, fax number, and telephone number
   Company identification
   Date
   Number of pages

Holiday Air, Inc.

P.O. Box 6958
Columbia, SC 29201-6958
(803) 555-0152

Current date

Ms. Ursula Pharr
MBA Managing Director
College of Business
Central University
Irmo, SC 29063-8447

Dear Ms. Pharr

Your request to provide six complimentary tickets for travel by your MBA Case Competition team was referred to our reservations group to determine if we could accommodate your request. The tickets to Montreal were requested for a departure on December 27 with a return on January 3. This holiday time period is our peak season, and demand is so high that we even had to block out tickets for our frequent fliers during this period. Therefore, we are unable to provide the complimentary tickets for this particular trip.

We would like very much to show our support for your MBA Case Competition team by offering the team six free tickets to any destination on our routes if the team has any other competitions scheduled during a nonholiday period. Just send me the information, and I will be happy to set up the tickets for another one of your competitions.

We wish your team success in this competition, and we look forward to having them aboard Holiday Air in the future.

Sincerely

Student's Name
Marketing Manager

Application 4C–2

Student's Name
Street Address
City, State, Zip Code

Current date

Ms. Renee Marks
Sales Manager
Resort Wear Boutique
6400 East Camelback Road
Scottsdale, AZ 85251-6973

Re: Order No. 395867

Dear Ms. Marks

Today I received a partial shipment of my order for two swimsuits and matching jackets that I purchased to take on a cruise. The shipment included the swimsuit of one set and the jacket of the other set. I was especially pleased with the swimsuit and look forward to wearing it on my cruise. However, I was disappointed to learn that the other items were back ordered and that I could expect them in approximately three weeks.

Because these swimsuit sets were ordered to take on a cruise that departs next week, the missing items will arrive too late to be of use to me. Therefore, I must cancel the order for the swimsuit and jacket that are back ordered, and I am returning the jacket that was shipped because I do not have the matching swimsuit.

I would appreciate a prompt refund of $94 so that I may purchase these items before I leave on the cruise.

Sincerely

Student's Name

ms

Application 4C–4

Raybon Construction Company
4309 West Third Street ■ Cleveland, OH 44113-7625
(216) 555-0139

Current date

Mr. David Scheatzle
Sales Representative
Custom Construction Software, Inc.
375 East Main Street
Aspen, CO 81611-9204

Dear Mr. Scheatzle

Several months ago, we purchased ConstructionEstimator software from you so that we could accurately estimate the amount of supplies needed for construction jobs. We have used the software to estimate the supplies needed on six different projects—three large and three small projects. On the three large projects, the software grossly underestimated the quantity of supplies needed. The result was just the opposite on the small projects; the software grossly overestimated the quantity of supplies needed.

These errors have been very costly. We had to pay restocking fees when we returned the excess supplies that were ordered on the small projects. On the large projects that were underestimated, we lost valuable time ordering additional supplies and waiting for them to be delivered. At our request, a technician from Custom Construction Software reviewed the procedures we used and verified that the software was used properly. Since ConstructionEstimator does not function properly, we wish to return it for a full refund of the $995 we paid for it.

We use several other software packages purchased from you and have been very pleased with them.

Sincerely

Student's Name

ms

Application 4C–6

Appliance **S**uperstore

7638 NW 34ᵗʰ Street
Miami, FL 33178-7025

Telephone (305) 555-0146
FAX (305) 555-0168

Current date

Mr. Arthur Rosenblaum
Rosenblaum Rental Properties
2442 South Bayshore Drive
Miami, FL 33133-7908

Dear Mr. Rosenblaum

Your request to increase your credit limit from $2,500 to $10,000 so that you can purchase appliances as needed for apartment units was received and carefully reviewed. Our decisions on credit limits are based on the applicant's level of income and credit record.

The $2,500 initial line of credit we extended to you about nine months ago was the maximum your income and your credit record justified at the time. During the last nine months, payments on your account have been late three times and did not meet the required minimum payments on two occasions. Therefore, we are unable to increase your credit limit at this time.

We will be happy to review a request for an increased credit limit after you have maintained your account satisfactorily for one year.

Sincerely

Student's Name
Credit Manager

ms

Application 4C–7

VanHuss Industries, Inc.
292 Crown Lake Drive ■ Hopkins, SC 29061-4736
(803) 555-0181

Current date

Ms. Carolyn Brandt
Manager, Customer Service
Holiday Air, Inc.
P.O. Box 6958
Columbia, SC 29201-6958

Dear Ms. Brandt

Last week when I returned from a business trip on Holiday Air Flight 485 from Atlanta to Charlotte, my luggage did not arrive on the same flight. The delivery service you provided dropped the suitcase off at the main desk of my company. When I picked up the $275 suitcase purchased less than six months ago, I noticed that it had been damaged badly. From the black tire marks on the bag, it appeared that the suitcase had been run over by the baggage trailer.

Your customer service representative instructed me to take the bag to Reggie's Repair Shop and have it repaired and billed to you. The repair job, however, was not satisfactory. Deep scars remain on the bag; therefore, it needs to be replaced. Reggie's Repair Shop indicated that I should contact you as Manager of Customer Service.

A copy of my receipt is enclosed. Please refund the $275 by the 15th so that I may replace the bag before my next business trip.

Sincerely

Student's Name

ms

Application 4C–9

VanHuss Industries, Inc.

TO: All Employees

FROM: Student's Name

DATE: Current

SUBJECT: Cafeteria Request

Providing appropriate facilities and services for all our employees is very important to us. Therefore, your request for a cafeteria with breakfast and lunch service was carefully considered. Breakfast and lunch service can be provided either through a full-service cafeteria or through an extended employee lounge.

A full-service cafeteria can be justified on a cost basis only when a large number of employees use the facility on a regular basis. Because the Kilgore facility has less than thirty employees, providing a full-service cafeteria is not cost effective. We can, however, expand and enhance the current employee lounge so that reasonable breakfast and lunch options will be available to employees.

The expansion work on the employee lounge is scheduled to begin immediately. A microwave oven and several vending machines with a variety of sandwiches, cereal packs, snacks, and beverages appropriate for lunch and breakfast will be added as soon as the work is completed.

We believe these enhanced facilities will meet your needs and improve our work environment significantly.

ms

Application 4C–8

VanHuss Industries, Inc.
292 Crown Lake Drive ■ Hopkins, SC 29061-4736
(803) 555-0181

TO: All Employees

FROM: Student's Name, Human Resources Manager

DATE: Current

SUBJECT: Request for Day-Care Center

VanHuss Industries designed its benefit package in an effort to meet the needs of all our employees. A number of you have requested that we review the benefits package and consider including a day-care center within company facilities. Approximately 30 percent of VanHuss employees have preschool children, and many are willing to pay a major portion of the child care costs. Therefore, we have investigated the option very carefully in an attempt to meet your needs.

During the investigation, a number of issues surfaced that relate to providing day care for dependents of employees. Obviously, a center must have competent employees capable of delivering high-quality care. Locating these employees appears to be a major problem. Issues of company liability that might result from the operation of the center are also involved. Finding appropriate space that could be adapted so that it will be suitable for the facility, having the budget to modify the space, and subsidizing the cost of operating the center are issues that must be resolved before any action can be taken on your request. Therefore, we have decided to appoint a committee to study the issue and, if a center is feasible, to make recommendations that can be used when next year's budget is being prepared.

The well-being of all our employees and their families is a high priority for our company, and we will give the committee's recommendations very careful consideration.

ms

Application 4D–2

VanHuss Industries, Inc.
292 Crown Lake Drive ■ Hopkins, SC 29061-4736
(803) 555-0181

TO: Jan Evans

FROM: Student's Name, Training Manager

DATE: Current

SUBJECT: Participation in Telecommunications Training Seminar

You requested and were granted permission to attend a two-day telecommunications training seminar offered by Southside Community College. The Training Department paid the $350 fee for your participation.

Last week, we received a $250 refund ($350 fee minus a $100 cancellation fee) from Southside Community College indicating that you did not attend the training seminar. Since we had no notification from you, we called Southside and verified that you did not participate or call to cancel your registration. Company policy requires that an employee who does not attend a scheduled training seminar must notify the Training Department and reimburse the company for any fees incurred unless the circumstances are beyond the control of the employee.

Please send me a $100 check made payable to the Training Department to cover the $100 cancellation fee charged by Southside Community College.

ms

c Lynn Adamson, Supervisor

Application 4C–10

Heritage Productions, Inc.
390 East Pearson Street
Chicago, IL 60611-9374
Telephone: (312) 555-0190
FAX: (312) 555-0146

Heritage Productions

Current date

FAX

Ms. Elizabeth M. Addison
Director of Product Development
Stonehedge Publishing Company, Ltd.
180 Piccadilly
London W1A 1AZ
England

Dear Ms. Addison

Thank you very much for your kind invitation to visit Stonehedge Publishing Company. Currently a new project is absorbing all my time. Therefore, I regret that I am unable to fit a trip to London in my schedule at the present time.

I believe that we have common interests in the English as a Foreign Language market that I hope we can explore in the future. When my schedule permits me to travel to London, I hope that you will once again invite me to visit Stonehedge Publishing Company. We would, of course, also welcome a visit from you if you have the opportunity to come to Chicago.

I look forward to the opportunity of meeting you on my next trip to London.

Sincerely

Gary Kiely, Manager
Research and Development Department

ms

Application 4E–3

Heritage Productions, Inc.

Heritage Productions

TO: Mr. Gary Kiely

FROM: Student's Name

DATE: Current Date

SUBJECT: Stonehedge Publishing Company

After analyzing a significant amount of material about Stonehedge Publishing Company and consulting with our marketing task force, I am confident that no compelling business reasons exist that would require you to make a special trip to London to visit Stonehedge publishers. In the future, opportunities may exist to work with Stonehedge Publishing Company.

Stonehedge does not compete directly with Heritage in the education or business markets. Stonehedge publishes EFL materials for elementary schools. Their primary products are textbooks. The videos they use to supplement the textbooks for elementary classes are tapes of entertainment programs in English rather than specially designed training tapes. The opportunity in the future is to explore joint video products with Stonehedge for EFL classes in elementary schools.

Stonehedge does not have business opportunities for us at the present time because of the following reasons:

- Business people in the countries Heritage is targeting prefer American English to British English and, of course, Stonehedge is a British publisher.
- Stonehedge has no experience in publishing for the business community, nor do they have distributors in the business market in the targeted countries.

The draft of the letter declining your invitation to visit Stonehedge at this time and a Fax cover sheet are attached. Please let me know if you need additional information or if you would like the letter modified in any way.

ms

Attachments

Application 4E–2

FAX

Heritage Productions, Inc.
390 East Pearson Street
Chicago, IL 60611-9374
Telephone: (312) 555-0190
FAX: (312) 555-0146

Heritage Productions

To: Ms. Elizabeth M. Addison

Fax: 071/836-5317

Telephone: 071/836-5823

From: Gary Kiely

Pages: 2

Date: Current

Application 4E–3B

---

390 East Pearson Street
Chicago, IL 60611-9374
Telephone: (312) 555-0190
FAX: (312) 555-0146

Heritage Productions, Inc.

Fax

To: Ms. Elizabeth M. Addison   **From:** Gary Kiely

Fax: 071/836-5317   **Pages:** 2

Phone: 071/836-5823   **Date:** Current

Re: Invitation   **cc:**

☐ Urgent ☐ For Review ☐ Please Comment ☐ Please Reply ☐ Please Recycle

• Comments

Application 4E–3B

PERSUASIVE LETTERS AND MEMOS

Chapter 5 opens on a different note than do previous chapters. This chapter begins with a focus on ethical issues. Class or group discussion in which students are asked to determine whether a particular situation is ethical or unethical is a good way to start a class that focuses on persuasion. Students will soon learn that not all cases are **either** ethical **or** unethical situations. Many times the issue depends on whose perspective is at stake. Examples of questions that might be used are:

1. Is it unethical or just good marketing for grocery stores to position candy in the checkout lanes so that children will have access to it while their parents are trying to check out?

2. If you are trying to sell your car, which you know has major mechanical problems, is it unethical to try to hide these problems from a potential buyer?

3. Is it unethical in a job interview for a prospective employer to embellish a job so that it sounds much better than the job actually is?

4. Is it unethical for a real estate agent to tell a prospective buyer that it is important to make an offer quickly because the owner has two other offers pending when the owner has no offers pending?

5. Is it unethical to try to persuade an athlete who has made a verbal commitment to play at another school (but has not signed the official letter of intent) to back down on the verbal commitment and make a commitment to your school?

Most students—somewhat reluctantly—will agree that the situations described in Questions 2 through 4 probably are not ethical. Most will think that 1 and 5 are ethical persuasion because the person was not manipulated, given dishonest information, or misled. It is important to point out to students that thinking about the ethics of situations is very important. Honesty and integrity are good business practices that pay off in the long run. You may get business one time by being dishonest, but you will never get repeat business once the individual learns about your lack of integrity.

Point out to students that in the earlier chapters their primary concern was on conveying information in an appropriate manner. Persuading someone to do something is a far more difficult task than conveying information in a sensitive manner.

PLAN EFFECTIVELY

The key issue that must be resolved before a persuasive letter is written concerns the appeal that is most likely to produce the desired results. Students often ask for things without thinking about their request from the reader's perspective. Forcing students to use empathy to determine if they would grant the same request if it were presented to them helps students to understand why analyzing the situation and determining the best appeal is important. Point out to students that the more costly a request is in time or financial resources, the harder it is to persuade the reader to grant the request.

Help the students understand the importance of credibility in getting a person to grant requests. A good example to use is a letter of application:

You include a statement on your résumé that you have good communication skills. However, in your application letter, you have grammar and spelling errors. What happens to your credibility? Is the employer likely to believe that you have good communication skills? If the employer thinks that statement is not accurate, is the employer likely to question the accuracy of other statements on your résumé?

The key point to make on appeals is this: A logical appeal works best when granting the request provides direct benefits to the reader. If no direct benefits accrue to the reader, a psychological appeal should be used. Refer students to the two illustrations on pages 118 and 119. Point out that the first one could have some direct benefit to the reader; therefore, a logical approach was included. In the second illustration, no benefit to the reader exists, or it is so indirect that it is not likely to be perceived as a benefit. Therefore, a psychological approach is appropriate for the second letter.

STRATEGY FOR PERSUASIVE MESSAGES

Point out to students that personal appeals work much better than mass appeals. Direct mail can be an example of a mass appeal. If a document looks like it has been sent to a mass of people, many individuals will see it as junk mail and throw it away without ever reading it. A document must be opened and read if a request is to be granted.

Getting attention is important; more important is that the attention should be favorable. Some techniques that get attention are not well received. Creativity is very important in designing appeals and gaining interest. The brainstorming exercise included in the chapter is a good one for students to use in a group setting. When students start analyzing ideas, what will appeal to one student may not be favorable to another. Doing a credibility check with a group produces different results than when one person tries to determine if an appeal is believable. The other advantage of group brainstorming is the piggybacking that one student can do from another student's ideas.

GLOBAL CONNECTIONS

In previous chapters, the emphasis on global communications was on being sensitive to cultural difference. This section discusses specific techniques to improve written communications that are sent to other countries. Some of the guides build on the general guides for writing that students learned in Chapter 2. The emphasis in a global communication setting is a more simplified approach, which lessens the chance of misinterpretation.

SAMPLE SOLUTIONS

The solutions presented in the instructor's manual illustrate one approach for solving the problems contained in the text. Student solutions may vary widely. The solutions provided in this manual or solutions prepared by the instructor can be used to provide feedback to students. They can be handed out or projected for students to compare to the solutions they prepared.

Review Guide 3: Present Ideas Positively (Page 121)

APPLICATION 5A

1. Please read all of the instructions carefully before completing the application.

2. Please call Judy to see if she needs extra help in getting ready for the meeting.

3. The specifications that you need to evaluate the proposal effectively are enclosed. We are sorry they were not included with the original document.

4. Please use only street addresses on our mailing labels because overnight delivery services require a street address rather than a post office box.

5. Jan did better on the math portion of the exam than on the verbal portion.

Editing and Language Arts Checkpoint (Page 122)

APPLICATION 5B

Refer to page 106 of Appendix B for the solution keyed to the language arts guides.

Writing Persuasive Messages (Pages 124–126)

APPLICATION 5C

Sample solutions for the ten exercises are on pages 53–56. Note that the scenarios expose students to the following industries:

- Advertising/public relations/marketing
- Manufacturing
- Technology
- Education/training

For the first three documents (exercises 1, 3, and 5) students are lead through a step-by-step planning process to give them experience in determining appropriate appeals and applying the writing strategies presented in the chapter. Then students are asked to plan and write additional documents independently.

1. Planning

    a. The direct benefit to Henderson & Henderson is very limited. The indirect benefit might come from being able to hire local graduates who have been trained using realistic materials and who are prepared to write effective messages. Psychological benefit would come from helping the local school system.

    b. The obstacles might be:
    - protecting confidentiality of materials
    - making sure that the company documents do not end up on the bulletin board as an example of bad writing
    - getting the materials to the instructor

    c. You can assure the firm up front that the confidentiality of the materials will be protected. Neither the company nor its clients will be identified in any communication. You can also offer to pick up the documents to simplify getting them from the company.

    d. A psychological appeal focusing on improving education will probably be the most powerful. A combination appeal focusing on improved education and pointing out the ability to hire graduates who are trained in effective writing would also be persuasive.

3. Planning

    a. VanHuss would have greater features with the new software than with the current proprietary software. The software could also be integrated very easily with other software applications that VanHuss is using. In addition, the software would be available now rather than having to wait for three to six months to get the upgrades.

    b. The Technology Task Force has ownership in the current software because they had it developed. Care must be taken not to imply that it was a bad decision. They also need to be convinced that the new software is better and does not cost more.

    c. Overcome the obstacles by focusing on the rapid speed at which technology is changing and the difficulty in keeping up with the changes. Point out that you get more features in less time at the same cost. Provide comparative features and cost data.

    d. A logical appeal will probably work best because direct benefits accrue to VanHuss Industries by making this decision.

5. Planning

    a. Changing the commission plan would make Hess more competitive in the job market because of candidates' concern about economic security. It would also help retain sales representatives in their first three years of employment. Having the same commission plan for all sales representatives would simplify the compensation system and be perceived as being more equitable for all representatives.

    b. The key obstacle that you have to confront is the perception that commission provides greater incentive than economic security. You would have to address the cost issue as well.

    c. You can overcome the obstacles by using a logical approach. You could provide data that show that you have lost candidates to competitors because of the compensation package and that you have more turnover in the early years in which compensation is based primarily on commission. Also, point out the concern about economic security that has been expressed by sales representatives in their early tenure. You can also point out that the total compensation would be about the same under either plan.

    d. A logical appeal would work because of the benefits for the company. A psychological appeal—particularly fear of losing out to competitors—would also help convince the Compensation Committee that the change is important. Perhaps combining the two appeals would produce the best results.

APPLICATION 5D

Self-Assessment (Page 127)

1. Short Answer

    a. The most appropriate strategy for writing a persuasive message often depends on how much persuasion is needed to move the reader to action. Usually, an indirect strategy works best because the reasons or justifications are presented before the request is presented.

        • Attract the reader's attention and interest.
        • Explain the request carefully, making sure that it is fully justified.
        • Minimize the obstacles and make it as easy as possible for the reader to act.
        • Request the desired action confidently.

b. The two types of appeals are logical appeals and psychological appeals. A logical appeal stresses to the reader that it makes sense to do something; that it is reasonable or rational. A logical appeal presents facts and supporting evidence, analyzes the facts, and draws logical conclusions.

A psychological appeal stimulates a reader's emotions. It is created when a reader feels that a request has inherent value. Psychological appeals make the reader feel good about doing something. They are often based on fair play and the importance of helping those less fortunate than we are.

c. A logical appeal is most appropriate when the request has direct benefits for the reader. A psychological appeal is most appropriate when the request has very indirect benefits or no benefits at all for the reader.

d. Credibility is important because convincing a reader to do something that he or she is not likely to do requires the reader to believe or trust the writer. Credibility is the key to achieving results when you are trying to persuade someone to do something. Both the writer and the message must be credible for good results to occur.

e. Ethical persuasion occurs when a writer uses techniques that are honest and forthright and does not mislead or manipulate the reader. Unethical persuasion occurs when the writer withholds information, presents misleading information, or intimidates the reader to take action that is not in his or her best interest.

C A S E   S T U D Y   APPLICATION 5E

Heritage Productions (Page 128)

This case application shifts the focus to an emphasis on culture and cultural differences between countries. A good way to start the discussion is to tell the students that they have just been notified that they will move to a new country in three weeks to spend a semester as an exchange student. Pick a country that they have not visited (do not use Malaysia because it is used in the text material). Ask students: What would you like to know about that country before you leave for a four-month stay? The answers will range widely. Examples of topics that probably will come up include:

- living conditions
- currency
- climate
- language
- kind of government as it relates to freedom, security, and so on
- food
- holidays
- cost of living
- health and safety issues
- customs of the people

What students ask for in the Malaysia case in the textbook will depend on what they find on the Internet. If they find information on holidays, governmental structure, population, and so on, they will not have to write for it. The most difficult topics to research are the customs of people. A number of books have been written on these topics, but they are not readily available on the Internet.

Malaysia was selected as the country in this application because business information is readily available and because it is not a country visited by large numbers of American tourists.

This application provides students with several different types of experiences. It focuses again on using on-line references to locate useful information. In this exercise, the emphasis includes checking the credibility of information located. Malaysia provided a good example because chat rooms and news groups have a large amount of information pertaining to discrimination. Some of the material is inflammatory. Students need to learn very quickly that much of the information in these types of settings is very biased and should not be assumed to be accurate.

The application also stresses to students that the way questions or requests are worded is important. Students need to inquire about information such as living conditions in a underdeveloped country in a very sensitive manner. A foreign address is used for one of the letters and an American address for the other to give students exposure to using foreign addresses. (Note that the same letter could be used for both requests.)

ETHICS QUESTION

The last component is an ethical issue for students to discuss. The scenario is that Heritage develops materials specifically for MetroMark and then talks about using those materials with other companies.

This practice is very common with custom-developed videos or training materials. The contracts should specifically state that the materials belong to their originator but are provided for the use of the specific company (MetroMark) and its employees. The contracts usually limit the company (such as MetroMark) from using the materials with other companies. As long as these conditions are understood up front, Heritage is not using the materials in an unethical manner. Without this provision, the cost of materials would be much higher. Heritage would use the same materials, with minor adaptations, for other companies. The benefit to the companies is that development of the materials costs less because the development costs are shared among several companies.

VanHuss Industries, Inc.

TO: Technology Task Force

FROM: Student's Name

DATE: Current

SUBJECT: Project Management Software

Several years ago the Technology Task Force took a bold step and had proprietary project management software developed for VanHuss Industries. That decision was a good one and gave us a competitive edge in the marketplace. Changes in technology have made our current software outmoded, and another bold decision is needed to give us a competitive edge once again.

We have analyzed our software to determine what changes must be made, and we have also analyzed software that is available on the market. Our analysis clearly indicates that purchasing the software now available on the market would be a better alternative than updating our current software. The key factors supporting this decision are:

- The software available for purchase outperforms our current software—it does everything our current software does and offers additional features as well.
- The software is part of the integrated suite of products that we currently use for word processing, spreadsheets, database, and graphics. Integrated project management output with documents produced using other applications would be greatly simplified.
- The software is available now whereas updating our current software would take three to six months.
- These extra benefits come at no extra cost. Costs for updating and costs for purchasing new software are comparable.

Please approve this request to purchase new software so that we can once again gain a competitive edge in technology.

ms

Application 5C–4

Midwestern University
College of Business Administration ■ Packer Hall
Oshkosh, WI 54901-2756

Current date

Ms. Martha Henderson
Henderson & Henderson
3862 Taft Avenue
Oshkosh, WI 54900-4762

Dear Ms. Henderson

Would you like to be able to hire employees who have been trained to write effective communications similar to those prepared in your company offices?

Industry is spending large sums of money training employees in basic communication skills. Our goal at Midwestern University is to teach students how to write effective communications before you hire them. To make sure our instruction is relevant, we are using actual samples of communications selected from leading organizations in our area.

Would you please share with us samples of letters, memos, and reports that are representative of communications in your company? Your company will not be identified in our instructional materials; and you may be assured that we will protect the confidentiality of your materials by changing names, addresses, and specific circumstances that would identify your company or clients.

We are putting together our instructional materials now, and it would be helpful if you could mail your samples to me in the enclosed envelope within two weeks. If you prefer, I could pick the communications up at your convenience. Together we can take action to improve the communication skills of our students and your prospective employees.

Sincerely

Student's Name
Business Communications Instructor

ms

Enclosure

Application 5C–2

Hess Industries, Inc.

TO: All Employees

FROM: Student's Name, Community Relations Manager

DATE: Current

SUBJECT: Community Chest Fund

Providing the basic needs for our families and loved ones is often taken for granted by those of us who are fortunate enough to have steady employment. However, many of our friends and neighbors in this community are not so fortunate. They are among the homeless, the hungry, the abused, and the neglected citizens who depend on the agencies supported by our annual Community Chest Fund to provide these basic needs. The enclosed brochure describes each of the more than fifty agencies supported by the Community Chest Fund.

Hess Industries is committed to being a good corporate citizen and to supporting our community in every way that we can. We participate with the other companies in our community in conducting a campaign within our workplace to help these needy citizens. To demonstrate our company's commitment, Hess matches every dollar that our employees give with an equal contribution to the Community Chest Fund.

We urge you to contribute generously to the Community Chest Fund.

ms

Enclosure: brochure

Application 5C–7

Hess Industries, Inc.
2948 Cloverdale Road ▪ Gadsden, AL 35903-7184
(803) 555-0183

TO: Compensation Committee

FROM: Student's Name

DATE: Current

SUBJECT: Commission Plan for New Sales Representatives

Our position in the market is conditioned upon hiring and retaining the best possible sales force. Recently that position has been jeopardized, and we have lost several candidates for sales positions to our competitors. The sales managers attribute these losses to the compensation package that we have, which is based primarily on commissions. Concern about economic security has caused many candidates to opt for jobs that provide security rather than taking the risk that comes with a commission-based position. We have also lost several employees to competitors for the same reason.

In light of current economic conditions, commission incentives may be working as disincentives. Therefore, we recommend that new sales representatives be placed on the same compensation plan as sales representatives with three years or more of tenure with the organization. This change would be perceived as being more equitable for all sales representatives. Changing the compensation base to 50 percent commission and 50 percent salary would not significantly affect the overall amount paid to sales representatives.

Please give careful consideration to this plan that will improve our ability to attract and retain the finest talent available.

ms

Application 5C–6

Hess Industries, Inc.

TO: Managers

FROM: Student's Name

DATE: Current

SUBJECT: Hess Leadership Institute

Hess Industries continually strives to meet the needs of our key employees. In response to numerous requests from many employees, Hess has contracted with the Topping Management Center of the College of Business Administration at Central University to develop an exciting certificate program entitled the Hess Leadership Institute. As a manager in a Grade 10 or higher position, you are eligible to participate in this excellent leadership development program.

The program consists of 8 three-day segments taken over a two-year period. Each participant will be enrolled in one segment per quarter. Four of the segments are core requirements that are taken by all participants. The other four segments are elected from ten alternatives designed to meet the specific needs of a variety of Hess managers. The program is conducted during the regular business day. Of course, Hess pays for all costs of the program including books and training materials. Key work-related assignments are completed between the segments offered.

We are pleased to be able to provide our employees with this outstanding opportunity to enhance their leadership potential and to earn the certificate offered. We encourage you to take advantage of this opportunity to enhance your career by enrolling in the program. Enrollment forms to sign up for the program are available in the Human Resources Office.

ms

Enclosure: Program Description

Application 5C–9

Computer Testing Associates, Inc.

4729 Preston Oaks Road ■ Dallas, TX 75240-2847 ■ (214) 555-0198

Current date

Dr. Karen Roskowski, Vice President
Office Systems and Services, Inc.
7900 Drake Avenue, S
Chicago, IL 60652-3049

Dear Dr. Roskowski

An ideal business venture is a mix of the right people, the right situation, and appropriate incentives to bring them together. We think we have the makings of an ideal business venture between Computer Testing Associates and Office Systems and Services.

Our goal is to establish CTA Training and Testing Centers in selected educational institutions in more than fifty cities. These centers would administer CTA-developed tests to full-time employees who would come to the educational institution to take these certification and skill validation tests. We believe that you and your associates are the ideal consultants to help establish these business partnerships. You are ideal because all your associates are educators who are well respected in their fields. Therefore, you would have far more credibility than sales representatives would have.

You will note from the enclosed proposal that we have offered incentives that we believe will make this an exciting project for you. The proposal offers, in addition to your standard fees, lucrative financial incentives for meeting the tight deadlines that are associated with this project.

Please give careful consideration to accepting this proposal. We believe you will be very happy that you did. The tight deadlines of the project make it necessary that we have your answer within one week. We look forward to hearing from you.

Sincerely

Student's Name
President

ms

Application 5C–8

MidSouth University
8097 Windy Hill Road ■ Decatur, AL 35503
(334) 555-0141

Current date

Ms. Yolanda DeShane
Human Resources Director
Hess Industries, Inc.
2948 Cloverdale Road
Gadsden, AL 35903-7184

Dear Ms. DeShane

One of my clients shared with me a copy of the compensation survey and the benchmark job descriptions that you recently sent to his company. The survey is constructed very effectively, and the job descriptions are very concise but descriptive. In fact, the survey is one of the best examples of a compensation survey that I have seen.

Would you please consider granting permission for me to use the survey and job descriptions as illustrations in the *Principles of Human Resources Management* textbook that I am writing. You would, of course, be given credit as the originator of the document.

Students would certainly benefit from studying the excellent examples that your materials would provide. I hope that you are willing to share these well-developed materials with them. I have enclosed a permission release form and stamped return envelope for your convenience, if you agree to my request.

Sincerely

Student's name, Professor
Human Resources Management

ms

Application 5C–10

The Woodworking Shop
3847 Indian Summer Point
Chapin, SC 29036-1847
(803) 555-0124

Current date

Mr. Roger Whetstone
246 Catawba Trail
Lexington, SC 29209-5178

Dear Mr. Whetstone

Placing a value on something is one of the most difficult things that we all have to do because of the special appeal that an item may have to an individual. A question we often have to ask ourselves when we have a choice of items is: Are the differences between the items really worth the difference in the price?

Your neighbor, Fred Baker, indicated that you are planning to have an entertainment center built in your home that is very similar to a custom-designed entertainment center you saw in our woodworking shop. Many custom-built items designed to meet the special needs of one room cannot be easily transferred to other settings.

Only a few homes can accommodate the large entertainment center you saw at our shop or the center you plan to build. Because the customer for whom our entertainment center was designed abandoned the project, someone will have an opportunity to save a tremendous amount of money on an entertainment center. That person could be you—if it meets your needs. You can purchase this beautiful entertainment center that was built at a contracted price of $3,500 for only $1,000, which gives us an opportunity to recover our expenses for the materials used in the project.

We invite you to visit our shop again and answer the question: Is the design of the entertainment center you want to build different enough that you would be willing to pay three to five times more for it than for the entertainment center you saw in our shop?

Sincerely

Student's Name

ms

Application 5D–2

Heritage Productions, Inc.
390 East Pearson Street
Chicago, IL 60611-9374
Telephone: (312) 555-0190
FAX: (312) 555-0146

Heritage Productions

Current date

American-Malaysian Chamber of Commerce
11.03 AMODA, 22, Jalan Imbi
Kuala Lumpur 55100, Malaysia

Ladies and Gentlemen

Our company specializes in preparing video programs designed to help
American families who are preparing for employment in or extended visits to
foreign countries. Currently we are working with several organizations who
plan to send a number of employees to work in Malaysia. I am in the
preliminary stages of collecting information about your country.

Could you please send us information about your country that would be
helpful to Americans who will have their first opportunity to visit your
country. Our citizens want to be able to understand and appreciate your
culture so that they can be gracious guests in your country. Information about
the following general topics would be particularly helpful:

- housing, food, and transportation
- currency
- climate
- languages spoken
- governmental structure
- holidays
- cost of living
- customs of the people

We would also appreciate any other information that you would like guests
visiting your country to know.

Sincerely

Student's Name
Assistant Manager

ms

Application 5E

LETTER AND MEMO REPORTS

Chapter 6 emphasizes the importance of writing effective messages for decision making. Many people visualize a report as a long, formal, analytical document. They do not think of letter and memo reports. Formal analytical reports, such as an annual report or a consultant's report, actually account for a relatively small portion of all business reports. A high percentage of all documents stay within a company, and that percentage includes documents used for decision making. Many of these internal documents are prepared in memo format, or if they are external documents, they are prepared in letter format.

Letter and memo reports differ from routine letters and memos in style and formality as well as in content. Reports tend to be researched carefully and written in a reasonably formal style. They tend to present both the positive and negative sides of issues so that an objective decision can be made. Most reports move upward in an organization. They are assigned to a subordinate employee (or team of employees) who, in turn, completes the report and directs the report back to the supervisor to use in making decisions. Employees are often judged by the quality of reports they write. Therefore, upward mobility can be enhanced by well-written reports and jeopardized by poorly written reports.

This chapter will provide many students with their first exposure to writing business reports. Students tend to find reports more difficult to write than other messages. To make the transition to writing letter and memo reports easier, the illustrations used are very simple, familiar topics that students can relate to. The same report is used to illustrate different organizational approaches and formats. Students can readily see that the report can be packaged in a number of different ways to accomplish different objectives.

The problems in this chapter have been intentionally structured so that instructors can use them for discussion about topics that relate to career development. Examples include the value of mentors and networking, social graces in an interview setting that includes a meal, and professional attire. Discussing these applications helps to lay the groundwork for the next chapter, which focuses on employment communications.

WRITING STYLE

Writing in objective style requires skill. Many students need a significant amount of practice to develop this skill. In Chapter 4, students learned to depersonalize messages involving sensitive situations or situations in which tact was needed. In this chapter, students learn that depersonalized communications appear to be more objective—thus, the name "objective writing style" is used for depersonalized communications.

Review the examples in the chapter comparing sentences written in personal and objective writing style. Additional sentences that can be used for illustration follow:

PERSONAL STYLE	OBJECTIVE STYLE
I interviewed six employees for 15 minutes each to determine their reactions to the training program.	Six employees participated in 15-minute interviews and shared their reactions to the training program.
I have analyzed all data carefully, and I believe that the program is cost effective and the results are good.	Careful analysis of the data shows that the cost-effective program produces good results.
I studied absenteeism in our company, and I found that our employees were absent most often on Mondays and Fridays.	The company absenteeism study documented that employees are absent most often on Mondays and Fridays.

Students often use passive voice when they convert sentences from personal style to objective style. Point out to students that objective style can be achieved using active voice—it just takes a little extra practice to develop the skill.

REPORT CONTENT AND FORMAT

Review with students the type of information that is normally contained in a report. Point out that headings may vary dramatically from one organization to another. The headings shown in the descriptive material in the chapter are topic headings—they describe the type of information included in the section. Wording may vary, however. Some organizations may prefer to use:

- Purpose (or Objective)
- Methods
- Results
- Conclusions
- Recommendations

In other organizations, the headings may be action oriented. They describe content rather than function. An example might be:

- Absenteeism Studied
- Employees Surveyed
- Absenteeism Related to Day of the Week
- Reasons Given for Absenteeism Questioned
- Plan Designed to Reduce Absenteeism

Students often have difficulty distinguishing between conclusions and recommendations. Conclusions are results obtained by analyzing and interpreting the data. Recommendations are a suggested course of action. The following example shows the difference in conclusions and recommendations:

Conclusion: *Effective Presentations* by Lee Martin meets the training needs and was the best of the six books reviewed.

Recommendation: The company should provide each participant in the training program with a copy of *Effective Presentations* by Lee Martin.

REPORT ORGANIZATION

The same logic students used in selecting the best strategy for writing positive, negative, and persuasive messages can be applied to selecting an organizational pattern for writing reports. Students can be taught how to decide which organizational approach to use for a report by having them ask three questions:

- What information must be conveyed?
- How will the reader(s) react to this information?
- What is the best approach to convey information in this particular situation, considering how the reader is likely to react?

Earlier, students learned to use a direct style for positive messages and an indirect style for negative messages. The same holds true for reports. Reports conveying good news are most effective when direct writing style is used. Reports conveying negative or controversial information are more effective when indirect writing style is used. Narrative and weighted approaches are simply variations of these two basic styles.

Encourage students to analyze the report illustrations carefully. They should refer to the illustrations when they try to apply the basic styles in the applications section.

GLOBAL CONNECTIONS

This application requires students to analyze material, make a decision, and prepare the report. It is designed to make students aware that a tremendous amount of information about the culture of a country is readily available at virtually no cost.

SAMPLE SOLUTIONS

The solutions presented in the Instructor's Manual (pages 62–66) illustrate one approach for solving the problems contained in the text. Student solutions may vary widely. The solutions provided in this manual or solutions prepared by the instructor can be used to provide feedback to students. They can be handed out or projected for students to compare to the solutions they prepared. Note that the scenarios expose students to the following industries:

- Manufacturing
- Publishing
- Education/training
- Service

APPLICATION 6A   *Review Guide 4: Write in a Clear, Readable Style (Page 145)*

1. An investigation of the causes of the assault showed that it could not have been anticipated or prevented.

2. Please send us the following information:

- Complete name, including middle initial
- Complete address, including street address, city, state, and postal code
- County in which you reside
- Social Security number
- Telephone number, including the area code
- Two credit card references

3. The morning and afternoon sessions of the Executive Committee meeting to discuss the location of the new facilities are scheduled in the Vista Conference Room. Lunch will be served in the Vista Dining Room.

4. The copy of the proposal you requested this morning is enclosed. Please let me know when you are ready to discuss it.

5. The manager notified employees that the company smoking policy was changed from a voluntary to a mandatory policy. Smoking is now permitted only in designated areas.

Editing and Language Arts Checkpoint (Pages 146–148)

APPLICATION 6B

Refer to page 107 of Appendix B for the solution keyed to the language arts guides.

Writing Letter and Memo Reports (Pages 149–151)

APPLICATION 6C

See pages 62–65 for sample documents.

Self-Assessment (Page 152)

APPLICATION 6D

1. Short Answer

   a. A personal style of writing includes the use of first and second person pronouns. An objective style of writing includes only third person pronouns and uses formal language.

   b. A deductive approach begins with the conclusions and then presents the supporting data to justify those conclusions. An inductive approach is just the opposite. It presents the supporting data, then lets those facts lead to logical conclusions.

   c. A direct approach is most effective when the reader is likely to agree with the conclusions and recommendations presented. An indirect approach is most effective when the reader is likely to disagree with the conclusions and recommendations presented. When the conclusion has not been presented, the reader is more likely to read with an open mind.

   d. A narrative approach presents events in the order in which they occurred. This approach is most effective when sequence makes a difference. A trip report would be an example in which a narrative approach works well.

   e. Conclusions are results obtained from analyzing and interpreting data. Recommendations are suggestions of what to do with the conclusions.

C A S E   S T U D Y   APPLICATION 6E

Heritage Productions (Pages 153–154)

See page 66 for a sample final report.

Bell Educational and Training Consultants

TO: Ms. Kerry Gallman
FROM: Student's Name
DATE: Current
SUBJECT: McKie Center Evaluation

Yesterday, I visited the McKie Center in Wilmington, Delaware, to determine its suitability as a VanHuss Authorized Training Center. I evaluated the location, facilities, equipment, staff, and the organization of the McKie Center.

McKie Center has two locations in Wilmington. I found the facilities to be excellent, and they are located in good areas of town. The equipment at the center is satisfactory. Two-thirds of the equipment is state of the art, and McKie has a replacement plan in place to upgrade equipment on a three-year cycle.

Larry McKie is the owner of the center. He has a staff of four managers (two center managers, a technical manager, and a training manager) and 15 employees. The center is organized effectively. Mr. McKie concentrates on strategic planning, business development, and marketing. Each center manager coordinates and schedules all training, and handles all registration and all financial record keeping. The center managers are also responsible for all administrative work. The technical manager is responsible for the training program, including designing, creating, and purchasing all training materials. The training manager also selects, hires, and trains the trainers and evaluates training sessions.

All members of the staff are well trained and already have the technical expertise VanHuss would need for its training program. I was very impressed with the professionalism and the technical expertise of the managers and their training staff.

I believe that the McKie Center is an excellent candidate to be a VanHuss Authorized Training Center. I recommend that you contract with McKie to establish a VATC at both locations in Wilmington, Delaware.

ms

Application 6C-1

Bell Educational and Training Consultants
3261 Moss Springs Road
Columbia, SC 29209–2948 ■ (803) 555–0183

Current date

Ms. Kerry Gallman, Director
Van Huss Industries
Training and Assessment Division
292 Crown Lake Drive
Hopkins, SC 29061–4736

Dear Ms. Gallman

The McKie Center is an excellent candidate to be a VanHuss Authorized Training Center. VanHuss should contract with McKie to establish a VATC at both locations in Wilmington, Delaware.

The site visit conducted yesterday confirmed that McKie has two excellent facilities located in good areas of Wilmington. The equipment is satisfactory. Two-thirds of it is state of the art, and McKie has a replacement plan in place to upgrade equipment on a three-year cycle.

Larry McKie is the owner of the center. He has a staff of four managers (two center managers, a technical manager, and a training manager) and 15 employees. The center is organized effectively. Mr. McKie concentrates on strategic planning, business development, and marketing. Each center manager coordinates and schedules all training, and handles all registration, and all financial record keeping. The center managers are also responsible for all administrative work. The technical manager is responsible for selecting, purchasing, and maintaining all hardware and software for both centers. The training manager has total responsibility for the training program, including designing, creating, and purchasing all training materials. The training manager also selects, hires, and trains the trainers and evaluates training sessions.

All members of the staff are well trained and already have the technical expertise VanHuss would need for its training program. The professionalism and the technical expertise of the managers and their training staff make the McKie Center an excellent candidate for a VATC.

Sincerely

Student's name
Consultant

ms

Application 6C–2

Century Technical Education Center

TO: Business Mentors

FROM: Student's Name

DATE: Current date

SUBJECT: Restaurant Recommendation

Local restaurants were analyzed to determine which ones would be appropriate to take a business client for dinner. The broad guidelines discussed in the last meeting were used as a guide in screening the restaurants. Information in the telephone directory, local advertisements, and recommendations from diners who had eaten at the various restaurants recently were used to screen the restaurants.

Restaurants were also contacted to ensure that they could accommodate a group of 12 at one table in a private room or two tables of six in the main dining room on Wednesday evening, March 20. Three restaurants met all of the criteria.

Chez Patrick

This small French restaurant would be appropriate for taking special clients out for a formal, elegant dinner. Both the food and the atmosphere are excellent. However, some clients may not be comfortable with the French menu. Entrees are priced at the upper limit of the business entertaining guides provided and all items are a la carte, making this restaurant quite expensive for business entertainment.

Daniel's Ribs

Generous servings of ribs and pasta are the primary features of this relatively informal restaurant. This restaurant has a nice atmosphere and would be appropriate for a relaxed evening in casual attire. Although the ribs and pasta are very good, they can be relatively messy to eat. Few alternatives are available for clients who may not like ribs or pasta. Prices are in the middle to upper middle of the acceptable range for business entertaining and include a trip to the salad bar and garlic bread.

Application 6C–3

Business Mentors
Page 2
Current date

The Riverside

This reasonably formal restaurant has a very nice atmosphere as well as very good food. The menu offers a large variety of seafood, veal, chicken, and beef items accompanied by one or two side dishes. Entrees are priced in the middle to upper middle of the acceptable range for business entertaining.

Conclusions and Recommendations

All three restaurants meet the basic criteria and would be acceptable for business dining. Of the three restaurants, *The Riverside* is recommended as the first choice because it offers a wide variety of menu items at reasonable prices and offers the appropriate environment for business entertaining. The other two restaurants offer a more limited menu. *Chez Patrick* has the disadvantage of being more expensive. *Daniel's Ribs* has the disadvantage of the risk of embarrassment that could result from eating messy food items.

A tentative reservation for two tables of six has been made in the main dining room of *The Riverside*. This reservation will be confirmed if the recommendation made in this report is approved.

ns

Application 6C–3

Candler Publishing Company

TO: Mr. Gary Douglas
FROM: Student's Name
DATE: Current
SUBJECT: Professional Attire

Problem

Currently, many employees of Candler Publishing Company dress in relatively casual attire. Concern was expressed about the possibility of casual dress creating an unprofessional image for the organization. The purpose of this report is to recommend an appropriate dress code for employees of Candler Publishing Company.

Supporting Data

Three data sources provided the information used to make judgments about appropriate attire for employees of Candler Publishing Company. The attire of employees in ten benchmark companies was observed. Clients and employees were given an opportunity to provide data.

Data Analysis

In eight of the ten benchmark companies observed, employees wore professional attire. In only two companies were employees observed wearing casual clothing such as jeans or jogging outfits. The attire varied depending on the position of employees. Managers and sales staff dressed very professionally. Men typically wore coats and ties; women typically wore business suits or tailored dresses. Attire worn by office staff was professional, but a little less formal than that worn by managers and sales personnel. People in technical positions tended to dress more casually than other employees. Most men wore slacks and shirts, and most women wore slacks or skirts and blouses. Some companies designate Fridays as days in which casual attire may be worn.

Clients were contacted to determine their preferences on attire worn in the office. The following chart shows the preferences of clients.

Client Preferences

15%   10%

75%

- ■ Professional
- □ Casual
- ▨ No Opinion

Application 6C–4

Mr. Gary Douglas
Page 2
Current date

Note that most of the clients contacted indicated they preferred to deal with companies whose employees had a professional appearance. This finding is particularly important because the companies with whom Candler Publishing Company likes to be compared (benchmark companies) tend to dress very professionally.

Employees provided a varied response when asked about appropriate attire. Many Candler employees felt that some Candler employees dressed too casually. Others liked the comfortable, if somewhat sloppy, attire worn at Candler.

Conclusions

Several conclusions were drawn from the data analyzed.

- Employees currently dress somewhat casually, which portrays a less than professional image.
- Employees at benchmark companies generally dress more professionally than employees at Candler Publishing Company.
- Clients indicated a strong preference for dealing with companies whose employees dressed professionally.
- Many, but not all, employees agreed with the assessment of clients about wearing professional attire.
- Managers and sales personnel in companies tend to dress more professionally than other employees.
- Many companies have casual dress days on Fridays.

Recommendations

The proposed general dress code for Candler divides employees into two categories--those who have contact with clients and those who do not have contact with clients. Employees with client contact should wear professional attire. Professional attire is defined as coats and ties for men, and business suits or tailored dresses for women. Employees who do not have client contact may wear more casual attire consisting of slacks and shirts with collars for men and slacks or skirts and blouses for women.

Fridays should be designated as casual dress days. T-shirts, shorts, and jogging outfits are not appropriate attire for the office on any days including casual days. Employees who are not meeting with clients may wear neat jeans on Fridays.

The attire recommended would enable Candler Publishing Company to project a more professional image that is comparable to benchmark companies and that meets the expectations of clients.

ms

Application 6C–4

Pat's Fitness Center

TO: Lynn Watson

FROM: Student's Name

DATE: Current date

SUBJECT: Weekly Report

This past week was the best week Pat's Fitness Center has had under the current management. Membership sales were outstanding. The following memberships were sold:

Lifetime memberships 4
Three-year memberships 6
One-year memberships 10

The participation rate was also very high. Facilities were utilized extensively, and programs drew good attendance as shown in the following summary:

- The weight room was used by 300 members.
- The handball and racquetball courts were used an average of nine hours per day.
- Three classes of aerobics were offered per day with an average attendance of 22 per class.
- Six special fitness programs were offered with an average attendance of 18 per program.
- Both the babysitting services and the vending operations continue to be profitable.

The demand for handball and racquetball courts continues to outstrip the number of handball and racquetball courts available for usage. The situation is especially critical during the peak demand time from 4 p.m. to 10 p.m. Expansion plans have been taken to three contractors for price estimates for building two more handball and two more racquetball courts. Bids are expected within ten days.

Overall, this week was an extremely successful one. A standard financial report for the week is attached.

ms

Attachment

Application 6D-2

Wexford Industries

TO: Ms. Lauren Adams

FROM: Student's Name

DATE: Current date

SUBJECT: Susan J. Walker, Wexford Industries MBA Fellowship Recipient

It was a pleasure to represent Wexford Industries at an outstanding fellowship event that provided wonderful public relations benefits for Wexford. The process for selecting the recipient of the $10,000 Wexford Industries fellowship was divided into two phases. The candidates were screened by Midtown University, and ten finalists were selected. Judges were provided with copies of the applications of the ten finalists one week prior to the on-campus interviews to select the recipient.

The judges for the final selection included a representative of Wexford as the sponsor of the fellowship. On Thursday evening, activities consisted of a get-acquainted dinner for the ten finalists, the judges, and administrators of the College of Business Administration. On Friday, the judges interviewed all ten finalists and ranked them on a point system. Then the judges met and agreed on the recipient.

The recipient, Susan J. Walker, was announced as the Wexford Industries MBA Fellowship recipient at a large reception Friday evening at the Faculty House. A copy of her biographical sketch is attached. She truly is an outstanding individual. The high caliber of all of the finalists, and the professional manner in which Midtown University conducted the entire event, made it a memorable one for everyone involved.

ms

Attachment

Application 6C-5

Comprehensive Reference Guide for Malaysia

Heritage Productions contracted to produce cross-cultural training videos for Malaysia in a cooperative venture with five other companies. Heritage also produces a concise training guide that participants can use for future reference. Two of the five companies participating in the cooperative venture initiated a request to prepare a comprehensive reference guide to accompany cross-cultural training videos.

Feasibility of Producing a Comprehensive Guide

The purpose of this study was to determine the feasibility and the desirability of producing a comprehensive reference guide. All five companies provided information about the need for a comprehensive guide.

Factors Analyzed

Key factors used in determining the feasibility of producing a comprehensive reference guide were the costs that would be incurred and the time required to produce the guide. Of the five companies in the venture, two indicated a strong desire to have a comprehensive guide. One company felt it would be nice to have, but that it was not a necessity. Two companies preferred not to have the guide if producing it resulted in increased costs or delayed the production time of the training videos. The availability of alternative materials was also considered.

Findings

Guides can be produced by the regular production team or can be produced by an external production house. The costs and the time frame vary depending on who produces the guide. The cost of producing a comprehensive guide rather than a regular guide is 10 percent higher if it is produced in-house and 20 percent higher if it is outsourced. The current production team has a full production schedule; therefore, producing the guide would result in a four-to-six week schedule delay. An external production house could produce the guide in the same time frame required for the regular guide.

Brochures and printed materials containing much of the information desired in the comprehensive guide are readily available and can be obtained in multiple copies. These materials may be an appropriate substitute for the comprehensive guide. They offer the advantage of being available at no cost, and using them would not alter the production schedule of the videos. A sample packet is attached for review.

Conclusions and Recommendation

The production of a comprehensive guide would increase costs and may delay the production of the videos; therefore, the regular guide should be produced. Companies should be provided with a sample packet of material along with a bibliography and instructions on how to obtain copies of the material if they wish to assemble packets for their employees.

Application 6E

Application 6E

FORM LETTERS AND MEMOS

Chapter 7 emphasizes the use of form messages to reduce the cost of communications. Students must be made aware that the cost of writing effective letters and memos is significant. A form message can be prepared for a fraction of the cost of an original message. Two types of time are involved in producing form letters—composition time and production time. Composition time is the most significant and the most costly part of the process. Once the form has been prepared, it can be used 50 or 100 or more times. Although it may take more time to compose an effective form or form paragraphs than it takes to compose an original letter, overall, major amounts of time are saved when the form is used over and over.

Another cost saving results from proofreading and editing time. Once form documents have been edited and checked for accuracy, they can be used over and over without proofreading them again. The downside, however, is if an error is not detected and corrected, it will appear each time the form is used. Therefore, careful proofreading of forms is extremely important.

USING FORMS EFFECTIVELY

Once students understand the importance of using forms for efficiency reasons, then it becomes important to stress to them that no matter how efficient a form might be, if it is not effective, it should not be used. Too often employees try to force a form to fit a situation that really is not appropriate. Some forms are flexible enough that they can be adapted.

Another important point to make is that form messages should not look like a form. Few people enjoy receiving documents that look mass produced. Mass-produced documents should be made to look as though they were custom-designed for the individual reading the document. The sophisticated word processing software that is available today makes it very easy to produce form documents that do not look like forms.

Also emphasize to students that they should make sure the letters and memos composed from form paragraphs flow smoothly. The only way to do this is to actually create letters and memos from the various paragraphs and read them to see how smoothly they flow. If they do not flow well, the paragraphs need to be edited to improve coherence.

The form provided in earlier chapters for assessing communications can be used effectively with form messages. A good teaching technique is to have students produce a letter from a variable form document and one from form paragraphs. Then have the students assess the effectiveness of the form using the same checklist that they have been using for original documents.

Assess Each Communication

1 **Does the communication accomplish its objective?**

A message is effective if it meet the needs of both the reader and the writer and is appropriate for the situation.

2 **Is the communication objective and logical?**

A communication should be factual, and decisions should be based on sound, logical reasons. The message should present adequate information to support the decisions made.

3 **Is the tone positive and confident?**

The message should convey the impression that the writer is knowledgeable and credible. It should build goodwill and focus on what can be done rather than on what cannot be done.

4 **Is the communication the right length?**

Only those ideas essential to conveying the message completely and effectively and to ensuring courtesy and building goodwill should be included. Ideas should be conveyed in a concise, but courteous manner.

5 **Is the message clear and easy to understand?**

A message is clear if the reader understands the message without having to reread any part of it. Sentences and paragraphs are reasonably short, and vocabulary is appropriate. Tables, illustrations, and graphic aids are used when appropriate to simplify content.

6 **Is the message coherent?**

The words, sentences, and paragraphs should be sequenced logically and flow smoothly. They should fit together to convey a message. Appropriate transitional words should be used to link ideas.

7 **Are important ideas emphasized?**

The reader should be able to discern which ideas the writer considers more important and which are less important than others.

8 **Does the communication have unity?**

The message should have a sense of wholeness; that is, the reader should be able to discern a beginning, middle, and end. All ideas in a paragraph should be related to one topic.

9 **Is the writing style effective?**

The message should be interesting and free of clichés, platitudes, and outdated expressions. It should convey a considerate, pleasant, and helpful tone that is appropriate for the situation.

10 **Does the message create a good image?**

The format and physical appearance should support the message, be consistent, and create a favorable impression.

SAMPLE SOLUTIONS

The solutions presented in the instructor's manual illustrate one approach for solving the problems contained in the text. Student solutions may vary widely. The solutions provided in this manual or solutions prepared by the instructor can be used to provide feedback to students. They can be handed out or projected for students to compare to the solutions they prepared.

Review Guide 5: Check for Completeness (Pages 163–164)

APPLICATION 7A

1. The information you should provide includes the advantages and disadvantages of converting from the Office Master suite to the Office Pro suite. You should include costs of doing so and time required to make the conversion. You must also request the permission needed. Assuming you have provided the information in the previous paragraph, you should anticipate the reader wanting to know what impact this proposed change would have on other employees and departments. Another issue would be who will train employees on the software and convert all the documents. Another issue may relate to whether some employees can keep the documents in the current version even though others convert them to the new software.

2. You should provide the date, time, location, and a complete schedule of activities. You should anticipate questions about appropriate attire, whether spouse, guest, or families are invited, whether attendees are expected to bring anything or do anything for the event, and whether any costs are involved.

3. You must provide information about the content and delivery method of the training program desired. The information would vary depending on whether this seminar is a new one or one that has been offered before. Dates desired and the length of the program must be provided. The Training Department needs to know how many employees will be involved and whether all of them can be trained at the same time.

   Questions should be anticipated about the costs and who pays them unless this is defined by company policy. Questions might also be anticipated about special problems that need to be addressed.

4. You should provide all logistical and schedule information.

   You should be able to assume that the managers know company policies about expenses, guests, and similar items.

   You should anticipate questions about who they will be meeting with and the type of business that will be conducted on this trip. You should also anticipate questions about preparation that must be done prior to the trip.

5. You should inform employees that the policy has been changed and provide the specific wording of the new policy and when it is effective. You should also provide the rationale for making the change. Including advantages and disadvantages would be helpful.

   You can logically assume that some smokers will be very displeased about this change and will want to know if their rights are being infringed on.

   You should anticipate questions relating to providing breaks to employees who have to go to another location in the facility to smoke—Must breaks be given? How long? How many?

Editing and Language Arts Checkpoint (Pages 165–166)

APPLICATION 7B

Refer to page 109 of Appendix B for the solution keyed to the language arts guides.

APPLICATION 7C

Writing Form Messages (Pages 167–169)

1. File: C7III-B3

Thank you for inquiring about Skilled Temps who can handle spreadsheet applications. We have Skilled Temps available who are trained and who have experience using all of the leading spreadsheet software packages. You do not waste your valuable time orienting our employees to your software. Skilled Temps begin productive work immediately.

File: C7III-B4

Thank you for inquiring about Skilled Temps who can handle database applications. We have Skilled Temps available who are trained and who have experience using all of the leading database software packages. You do not waste your valuable time orienting our employees to your software. Skilled Temps begin productive work immediately.

2–7. Sample solutions for the 7 exercises are shown on pages 71–73. Note that the scenarios expose students to the following industries/career fields:

- Retail/Credit and Collection
- Manufacturing/Human Resources
- Medical/Health/Sales
- Education/Training
- Business Services/Temporary Employment

APPLICATION 7D

Self-Assessment (Pages 170–171)

1. Short Answer

   a. Complete forms are identical letters or memos sent to multiple individuals. The advantages of complete forms are that they are efficient and they are very cost effective. The disadvantage is that the complete form is not personalized in any way.

   b. Variable forms are documents with minor variations in content that can be sent to multiple individuals. The advantages are that they are efficient, cost effective, and personalized. The disadvantages are that they take a little more time to develop and to prepare than do complete forms.

   c. Form paragraphs are a series of stored paragraphs that can be combined with the appropriate opening and closing letter or memo components to create documents. The advantage of form paragraphs is that they offer tremendous flexibility in meeting specific needs. The disadvantage is the difficulty of designing and developing paragraphs that fit together and flow smoothly.

   d. Guide forms are samples or models that employees can use as a guide in writing messages. The advantage of guide forms is that they are effective original messages tailored to meet the needs of the reader. The disadvantages are that they are time consuming and costly and they require the person producing the forms to have good communication skills.

See page 74 for sample solutions to 7D-2 and 7D-3.

APPLICATION 7E   C A S E   S T U D Y

Heritage Productions (Page 172)

See page 75 for a sample solution.

VanHuss Industries, Inc.

9081 Packer Drive · Green Bay, WI 54304-2536
(414) 555-0150

<Date Code>

<Title> <First Name> <Last Name>
<Position>
<Company>
<Street Address>
<City>, <State> <Postal Code>

Dear <Title> <Last Name>:

<Applicant> has applied for a position as a <position> with us and has listed you as a reference. We would appreciate your help in evaluating this applicant.

Please provide us with the information requested on our enclosed standard evaluation form and return the completed form to us in the enclosed envelope. We hope you will provide as much information about this candidate as you possibly can. Our goal is to make a decision within two weeks; therefore, we would appreciate hearing from you soon.

Sincerely

Student's Name
Personnel Assistant

ms

Enclosure

Application 7C–3

Skilled
Temps
Inc.

1654 Highland Road   Dallas, TX 75218-2059
(214) 555-0134

Current date

Ms. Elizabeth Davis
Clearwater Industries
4938 Maple Walk Street
Humble, TX 77346-5802

Dear Ms. Davis

Thank you for inquiring about Skilled Temps who can handle database applications. We have Skilled Temps available who are trained and who have experience using all of the leading database software packages. You do not waste your valuable time orienting our employees to your software. Skilled Temps begin productive work immediately.

All Skilled Temps complete extensive assessments and are certified as having mastered specific skills before they are placed on a job. This certification program enables us to match your job requirements with the skill levels of our employees. We keep a profile of your company on record that describes the skills you require and the type of work to be performed. Changes in the profile can be made any time you request service.

The enclosed brochure provides complete job descriptions and a cost schedule. One of our representatives will telephone you next week to answer any questions that you may have about Skilled Temps.

Sincerely

Student's Name
Corporate Placement Director

ms

Enclosure

Application 7C–2

VanHuss Industries, Inc.
9081 Packer Drive · Green Bay, WI 54304-2536
(414) 555-0150

Current date

Mr. Marcus Schwartz
Marketing Manager
Midtown Medical Supplies
3958 Ridgecrest Street
Las Cruces, NM 88005-1486

Dear Mr. Schwartz

Kenneth W. Willis has applied for a position as a sales representative with us and has listed you as a reference. We would appreciate your help in evaluating this applicant.

Please provide us with the information requested on our enclosed standard evaluation form and return the completed form to us in the enclosed envelope. We hope you will provide us much information about this candidate as you possibly can. Our goal is to make a decision within two weeks; therefore, we would appreciate hearing from you soon.

Sincerely

Student's Name
Personnel Assistant

ms

Enclosure

Application 7C-4

Travel Master Shop
P.O. Box 5284 · Beverly, MA 01915-5284
(617) 555-0110

Current date

Ms. Roseanne Desselles
12 Essex Street
Beverly, MA 01915-3867

Dear Ms. Desselles

Success in any endeavor is dependent on making good decisions. You made an excellent decision when you purchased your new luggage from the *Travel Master Shop*. Travel Master decided more than twenty years ago to provide our customers with the finest travel products available at a reasonable price. And that decision is one of the primary reasons we have been successful for so many years.

Until now you have always made excellent decisions on the way you maintained your account with us. However, your $2,290 account is now more than three months past due. We hope you will make another excellent decision—the decision to protect your fine credit rating.

You can do so by sending us your check for $2,290 in the enclosed envelope. Please take action now.

Sincerely

Student's Name
Credit Manager

ms

Enclosure

Application 7C-5

Video Productions Inc.

1847 Main Street
Columbia, SC 29201-4738
(803) 555-0114

<Date Code>

<Title> <First Name> <Last Name>
<Position>
<Company>
<City>, <State> <Postal Code>

Dear <Title> <Last Name>

Thank you for ordering <name of training program>. The videocassettes for Modules 1 and 2 are enclosed. We are confident you will be pleased with the quality of our training and will find it to be very beneficial to your employees.

The videotapes on which the program is recorded are high-quality tapes designed for extensive use. They are carefully checked prior to shipment. However, should a tape be defective or damaged in shipment, it will be replaced immediately if it is returned within two weeks of receipt of the tapes. Worn-out or damaged tapes will be repaired or replaced within one year from the date of purchase at a cost of 25 percent of the current catalog price. The damaged tape must be returned with your request for reimbursement. The video programs are protected by copyright and may not be videotaped, duplicated, or copied in any form or medium.

Please call us if you need additional copies or if you would like us to develop custom-designed materials for your organization to complement the program. Thank you again for ordering <name of training program>.

Sincerely

Student's Name
Marketing Manager

ms

Enclosure

Application 7C-6

Video Productions Inc.

1847 Main Street
Columbia, SC 29201-4738
(803) 555-0114

Current Date

Mr. Jody Swinney
Training Manager
Sports Marketing, Inc.
3748 Devine Street
Columbia, SC 29209-3847

Dear Mr. Swinney

Thank you for ordering *The Art of Negotiating.* The videocassettes for Modules 1 and 2 are enclosed. We are confident you will be pleased with the quality of our training and will find it to be very beneficial to your employees.

The videotapes on which the program is recorded are high-quality tapes designed for extensive use. They are carefully checked prior to shipment. However, should a tape be defective or damaged in shipment, it will be replaced immediately if it is returned within two weeks of receipt of the tapes. Worn-out or damaged tapes will be repaired or replaced within one year from the date of purchase at a cost of 25 percent of the current catalog price. The damaged tape must be returned with your request for reimbursement. The video programs are protected by copyright and may not be videotaped, duplicated, or copied in any form or medium.

Please call us if you need additional copies or if you would like us to develop custom-designed materials for your organization to complement the program. Thank you again for ordering *The Art of Negotiating.*

Sincerely

Student's Name
Marketing Manager

ms

Enclosure

Application 7C-7

VanHuss Industries, Inc.

To: Siu-Ki Kwok
From: Student's name
Date: Current Date
Subject: Your Travel Request

Your travel request has been received and reviewed. The request has been processed, but modifications in the request were required because the request did not fully conform to the travel policies established by the Executive Committee of VanHuss Industries.

The changes made on the travel request are highlighted on the enclosed copy of the Travel Request form. These changes were made to lower the total cost of the trip as mandated by VanHuss travel policies. Please call immediately for an exception if the revisions present a hardship or would have a negative effect on the purpose of the trip.

Your tickets and the confirmation for any other services required will be delivered to you at least two days prior to departure. Any changes made in the travel arrangements should be made through the Corporate Travel Department. Please remember that restricted tickets are used and that any changes made in your travel plans may result in penalties.

ms

Enclosure

Application 7D–3

C7D-MH

To:
From:
Date: Current Date
Subject: Your Travel Request

C7D-B1

Your travel request has been received and reviewed. The request has been processed, but modifications in the request were required because the request did not fully conform to the travel policies established by the Executive Committee of VanHuss Industries.

C7D-B2

Your request for international travel has been received and reviewed. However, the travel request cannot be processed because VanHuss travel policies require that all international travel requests be signed by a senior vice president.

C7D-M1

The changes made on the travel request are highlighted on the enclosed copy of the Travel Request form. These changes were made to lower the total cost of the trip as mandated by VanHuss travel policies. Please call immediately for an exception if the revisions present a hardship or would have a negative effect on the purpose of the trip.

C7D-M2

An Exception to Travel Policy form is enclosed. Please return the form with the signature of the appropriate senior vice president. I will process your travel request just as soon as I receive the signed form.

C7D-E1

Your tickets and the confirmation for any other services required will be delivered to you at least two days prior to departure. Any changes made in the travel arrangements should be made through the Corporate Travel Department. Please remember that restricted tickets are used and that any changes made in your travel plans may result in penalties.

Application 7D–2

Country Information

People

The people of Malaysia are known as Malays or Malaysians. Malaysia has a diverse population consisting of several large ethnic groups, including Malays, Chinese, and Indians, and a number of smaller ethnic groups. Malay (also known as Bahasa Malaysia) is the primary language, but English is used extensively for business purposes. Chinese and a number of dialects are also spoken. The primary religions in Malaysia include Muslim, Buddhist, Hindu, Christian, Confucian, and Taoist. Many country customs are a product of religious traditions.

Malaysia has a population of almost twenty million people. The Peninsular Malaysia is densely populated with a concentration of more than three-fourths of the Malaysian population. Other areas are not as densely populated.

Geography

Malaysia is a country with two separate land regions consisting of a little more than 127,000 square miles. One region (Peninsular or West Malaysia) is located in Southeast Asia, and the other region (East Malaysia) is on the northern coast of Borneo. Kuala Lumpur, the capital of Malaysia, is the largest city. Other cities include Georgetown, Kelang, Johor Baharu, Melaka, Kuching, and Kota Kinabalu.

The climate is tropical. The coastal plains contain swamps and marshes; the interior sections contain tropical jungles and mountains. The heavy rain, or monsoon, season begins around October and usually lasts until March.

Government

Malaysia's government is a constitutional monarchy with a ceremonial ruler called a king. Malaysia has thirteen states and one federal territory. The king is elected every five years from the sultans of the Peninsular Malaysian states. Parliament includes a Senate and House of Representatives. The legal system is based on English common law.

The United States and Malaysia have good relations. The government is proactive toward development and industrialization. Conditions are favorable for both domestic and international business.

Application 7E

Page 2

Economy

The major industries are manufacturing and agriculture. The primary crops include palm oil, natural rubber, timber, cocoa, and pepper. Tin is a major industry in Malaysia. The largest economic sector is manufacturing. The leading products include electronic components, particularly semiconductor devices, textiles, apparel, and air conditioners. Malaysia has almost full employment, and labor relations are good. The Ringgit is the monetary unit. Malaysia has very few limitations on currency exchange.

Customs

Information on customs will vary significantly depending on the sources used. Students may list eating customs, gestures with hands, greeting customs, ways to address people, religious customs, and a variety of other customs.

Sources for information will probably include government agencies, embassy, Internet, geography books, travel references, and books on customs of various countries.

Application 7E

CHAPTER

8

COLLABORATIVE AND TEAM WRITING

Chapter 8 emphasizes the importance of teamwork in organizations. Today, many organizations assign major projects to teams rather than to individuals. With large projects, the teams are usually cross-functional. Representatives of the key areas of the company have input in the projects. It would not be uncommon for a cross-functional team to have a representative from areas such as development, production, marketing, legal, human resources, finance, and senior administration. Cross-functional teams enhance the flow of communication throughout the organization and bring in a variety of perspectives. Usually, long reports are prepared at the conclusion of the project to send up the chain of command for approval.

This text focuses on basic communications rather than on long, formal, analytical reports. This chapter is designed to lay the groundwork for these more advanced communication responsibilities. The focus is on helping students develop the skills needed to work in teams, to solve problems, and to communicate those solutions.

This whole chapter focuses on a team approach to solving problems and writing messages. The materials could be handled by individual students; however, they would miss the collaborative work portion. If you appoint teams, try to make them as diverse as possible. Point out to students that the more diverse the team is, the less likely they are to succumb to "groupthink." In addition, learning to work with diverse groups is a very important career skill.

Remind students to apply the problem-solving and brainstorming guides they learned in Chapters 1 and 2 to discuss the issues. Point out that the team should first determine the base of knowledge the team has. Then the team needs to collect additional information from a variety of sources to supplement what they have been able to pool. Once the information is available, it should be analyzed and discussed to determine the best alternatives.

Another key point to emphasize is that current technology really facilitates group work. Many schools will not have groupware available to show students. However, students can work with the annotations, comments, and revisions features of word processing software to collect comments from several team members. An illustration is included on the template disk.

Most of the problems in this chapter consist of memos reporting group consensus about various issues that students were asked to discuss. Because of the nature of the problems, the memos written by different teams may vary dramatically. The same is true for the solutions provided. Encourage students to use an efficient writing style. Most of the memos lend themselves to enumerations that can be numbered or presented with bullets.

Review Guide 6: Use an Efficient, Action-Oriented Style (Page 179)

APPLICATION 8A

1. The committee reviewed the report, but they postponed taking action on it until the next monthly meeting.

2. The Action Council sent the mayor of Gilbert and the governor of Texas checks for $100 to assist in their campaigns for reelection.

3. The staff encouraged Pat to consider options in addition to the three vendors' proposals.

4. Please announce that if the team loses, it will return home after the game.

5. Terry was asked to repeat the information about the maximum amount that could be earned without losing retirement benefits.

Editing and Language Arts Checkpoint (Pages 180–181)

APPLICATION 8B

Refer to page 110 of Appendix B for the solution keyed to the language arts guides.

APPLICATION 8C

Collaborative and Team Writing (Page 182)

Sample solutions for the five documents are on pages 79–83. Note that the scenarios require students to work as teams. The team should use brainstorming techniques, collect external information, make decisions, and report their findings effectively. Scenarios have been designed that have no one best way of accomplishing the results. Because the topics can be approached from different perspectives, you should expect considerable variation in the documents produced by the different teams in your class. In fact, discussing the differences produced by the teams would be a very valuable learning experience. An additional team activity could be to constitute new teams consisting of one person from each team in the class and give them the assignment of taking the memos of all the teams and consolidating them into one final summary memo.

The content of the scenarios in this chapter are designed to integrate basic business practices that are important to working successfully in a business environment. Topics such as voice mail, telephone techniques, time management, effective meetings, and effective visuals are used in this team project so that students will discuss and research them. Many of the "soft skills" that are critical SCANS competencies are embodied in these topics. Ensure that students understand their importance in the business world and take them seriously.

APPLICATION 8D

Self-Assessment (Page 183)

1. Short Answer

   a. Different types of teams in organizations include teams within a work unit, cross-functional teams, teams with formal leaders appointed, and leaderless teams.

   b. Organizations achieve synergy by working with teams. The results produced by the team are better than the work that could be produced by any individual. Bringing people together with different perspectives improves decision making and facilitates communication in the organization.

c. Team members should have good problem-solving skills, good interpersonal skills, and the ability to communicate in addition to the content skills required for the situation.

d. To ensure content consistency, the team should develop a comprehensive outline and determine who will handle each part to ensure that nothing is left out and that items are not duplicated. The team should also agree on the level of detail, and the writing style and should ensure that sections fit together. One way to do that is to use a consistent pattern for opening and closing each section.

e. To ensure mechanical consistency, the team should determine the layout and stylistic elements that will be used prior to writing the document. Elements that must be considered include fonts, margins, layout, headings, headers and footers, and pagination style.

APPLICATION 8E   C A S E   S T U D Y

Heritage Productions (Page 184)

Ask students to describe the number of characteristics they ended up with on their list. Discuss with them the process they used to reach agreement on the ten most important characteristics. Emphasize to them that they should not vote on the items listed, but that they should discuss each item and give reasons why one characteristic may be more important than another. Efforts to reach agreement produce better results than voting to determine what to include or eliminate.

Suggest to students that they might want to include a brief description of the process in the memo to Mr. Garrison.

See page 84 for a sample solution.

VanHuss Industries, Inc.

TO: Staff Development Committee

FROM: HRM Team

DATE: Current date

SUBJECT: Effective Meetings

Some of our department members indicated that efforts should be devoted to making all meetings more effective. Meetings are both time consuming and costly; therefore, the HRM Team agreed to study ways to improve meetings and to share those results with you.

In addition to our own input, we consulted with a number of other VanHuss Industries employees to gain their perspective on company meetings. We also used the Internet and our library to access information on the topic. After examining all the information, the team agrees that meetings can and should be more effective. Recommendations for improving meetings are summarized below.

Recommendations for Making Meetings Effective

1. Ensure that the right people participate in the meeting. Everyone who needs to be at the meeting should be invited to the meeting. If people who must provide needed information are not present, time will be wasted.
2. Provide participants with an agenda prior to the meeting. The agenda should put individuals on notice to be prepared to discuss the items listed. Individuals who have a specific responsibility at the meeting should be notified ahead of time and clearly informed of what is expected of them. They should also know how much time is allocated to each section of the agenda.
3. Stick to the agenda and the time schedule. Ask people contributing information that is not pertinent for the discussion to hold that information and put it on the agenda of a future meeting.
4. Encourage everyone to participate actively and openly; discourage anyone from dominating the meeting.
5. Summarize the actions agreed on and end on time.

We believe these few suggestions will improve meetings for all of us.

ms

Application 8C–1

VanHuss Industries, Inc.

TO: Staff Development Committee

FROM: HRM Team

DATE: Current date

SUBJECT: Uses and Abuses of Voice Mail

The HRM Team studied the effective use of voice mail. The following information summarizes what we believe to be effective uses of voice mail and what constitutes abuses of voice mail.

Effective Use of Voice Mail

- Use voice mail for hours during which the office is closed.
- Use voice mail as a backup only when you cannot answer the telephone and other team members are unable to answer the telephone for you.
- Leave a short, clear recording for callers. Update the message frequently and provide options to reach an operator.
- Check voice mail frequently and return calls immediately.
- Train repetitive callers to use voice mail effectively—teach them to leave a message that indicates the purpose of the call and specific information you need in order to respond to them effectively.
- Be prepared to leave a message on voice mail when you call customers.
- Plan a message prior to calling so that you can be effective if you reach voice mail rather than the individual.
- When you respond to voice mail, have the information or the solution requested in the message.
- Check your attitude before you use voice mail.

Abuses of Voice Mail

- Use voice mail to "screen" calls while you are in the office and available to take calls.
- Let calls roll over to voice mail so that you can get paperwork done.

Staff Development Committee
Page 2
Current date

- Answer voice mail messages "when you get around to them."
- Respond to voice mail messages without the information or solution requested when it is possible to provide the information.
- Call customers when you know they will be out of the office so that you can leave a message rather than talk with them.
- Leave long recorded messages that provide for all options that a person might encounter rather than limiting the message to key options that are used frequently.
- Let the customer know how much you dislike voice mail.

Voice mail is a very valuable tool if it is used in an effective manner. The most important thing to remember is that a caller would rather talk with you than with a recording device.

ms

Application 8C–2

VanHuss Industries, Inc.

TO: Staff Development Committee

FROM: HRM Team

DATE: Current date

SUBJECT: Keys to Effective Telephone Calls

The telephone generates a major portion of the business conducted by VanHuss Industries; therefore, using it effectively makes good business sense. The HRM Team explored ways that employees could be more effective in dealing with customers on the telephone.

Most people take the telephone for granted because they have used it extensively for many years. Yet the telephone creates many complaints for customers of most companies. Key complaints that customers have include playing telephone tag, being transferred from one area to another, having to hold, dealing with rude people on the telephone, and being interrupted while they are talking to employees. Employees also complain extensively about the telephone. The primary complaints employees make are having their work interrupted, trying to answer multiple lines ringing at once, and having difficulty in communicating with some people on the telephone.

Keys to Effective Telephone Calls

To be more effective on the telephone, employees should:

- Answer the telephone promptly and set the tone for a professional conversation. The keys to setting a professional tone include identifying VanHuss Industries and yourself, projecting your voice, sounding alert, and being warm and friendly.
- Establish credibility and expertise immediately. The keys to establishing credibility include getting factual information quickly and verifying to the customer that your information is accurate, responding to the customer in a way that demonstrates that you know your job and you are knowledgeable about the customer's situation, and conveying the attitude that you can produce results for the customer.

Staff Development Committee
Page 2
Current date

- Listen empathetically and let the customer know that you are listening and that you understand what the customer is saying. The keys to listening empathetically are to focus total attention on the customer, supply verbally the feedback the customer would observe in a face-to-face situation, and use noninterrupting confirmers ("yes, sure, OK") to let the customer know you are listening, you understand, and you agree.
- Use effective questioning techniques. The keys to questioning effectively are to use open-ended questions when the customer is upset or wants to explain the situation and to use close-ended questions to get factual information quickly.
- Summarize key points and end the conversation on a friendly note. The keys to ending a conversation effectively are to ensure that both parties understand exactly what was agreed to during the conversation and to ensure that the customer leaves the conversation with a feeling of their needs being satisfied.
- Follow up with required action. The keys to concluding a telephone conversation successfully include taking the action promised during the conversation and making appropriate notes for future reference.

Effective use of the telephone is good business for VanHuss Industries. A conscious effort to be more effective on the telephone will produce good results.

ms

Application 8C-3

Application 8C-3

VanHuss Industries, Inc.

TO: Staff Development Committee

FROM: HRM Team

DATE: Current date

SUBJECT: Guides for Preparing Effective Visuals

Visuals help to support a presentation and enhance learning. The type of visual support that works best depends on the objectives of the presentation. Both projected and nonprojected visuals enhance a presentation. Nonprojected visuals include models, products or other objects, handouts, and flip charts. Projected visuals include transparencies, computer visuals, slides, and video. Visuals should support rather than replace a speaker. Speakers should use visuals that they can control easily.

Because projected visuals are used in the orientation and training program, the HRM team researched guides for preparing effective projected visuals.

Guides for Preparing Effective Visuals

Unity. All the content on a visual should relate to one topic. Unity on a visual gives a sense of wholeness.

Simplicity. A visual should be uncluttered and free of distracting elements. Simplicity makes a visual easy to understand. A viewer should be able to look at a visual and understand it very quickly.

Economy. The amount of copy on a visual should be limited. Lines should have no more than four or five words, and a visual should have no more than five or six lines. Words and phrases are more effective than full sentences. The speaker provides the full sentence; the phrases provide visual cues to support the speaker.

Consistency. The style, layout, and content of visuals in a presentation should be consistent. Visual elements such as lines, bullets, and other attributes should be consistent from one visual to the next. Writing style should be consistent. For example, if one bulleted item on a visual begins with a verb, all bulleted items on that visual should begin with a verb.

Application 8C–4

Staff Development Committee
Page 2
Current date

Readability. The audience must be able to see and read the content of a visual. Font size and drawings should be large enough that the entire audience can read it easily. Color also affects readability. Some colors project better than others. A sharp contrast between the type color and the background color enhances readability.

Clarity. The content on a visual must be clear. A viewer should be able to look at the visual and very quickly understand the meaning that is intended. Complicated, confusing visuals hinder rather than help a speaker.

Interesting. A visual should be designed to command attention and hold the interest of the audience. Effective use of color, charts, graphs, or clip art can help to make a visual more interesting.

Visuals are beneficial to both the listener and the speaker. Therefore, the time spent developing effective visuals is a very good investment of time.

ms

Application 8C–4

VanHuss Industries, Inc.

TO: Staff Development Committee

FROM: HRM Team

DATE: Current date

SUBJECT: Feasibility of Using International Teams

The HRM Team was asked to research the possibility of using an international team to work on a major customer service training program. The issue was approached from the perspective of the benefits gained by adding international members, the problems that result from the geographical distance involved, and ways to minimize the problems inherent in working with an international team.

The benefits of an international team are significant. VanHuss Industries is an international company with operations in a number of foreign countries. The expectation of customers varies significantly depending on the culture of the country. Having representatives of different countries on the team would expand the perspective and knowledge base of the team. The foreign team members would bring to the discussion information that the American team members would not possess.

Working with teams in different geographical areas would present challenges. To have face-to-face meetings, international travel would be involved for three members. International travel involves significant cost and time. Input from foreign team members could be provided by other means including video conferencing, computer conferencing, telephone conferencing, and E-mail or fax.

Language would not be a significant problem because VanHuss conducts all business in English. However, difference in language, customs, and backgrounds would make communicating effectively a challenge. However, it would be good preparation for dealing with customers who have these same communication challenges. Learning more about the cultures and using technology effectively would minimize some of the problems that result from diversity.

Because the customer service program is a major one, it is worth the effort to do what is necessary to make an international team work. The benefits accrued from using a diverse team far outweigh the problems that are inherent in working with a culturally diverse team.

ms

Application 8D-2

VanHuss Industries, Inc.

TO: Staff Development Committee

FROM: HRM Team

DATE: Current date

SUBJECT: Guides for Managing Time Effectively

The team researched ways to manage time effectively. Time is an interesting concept to study because it is one of the few resources that is distributed equally; no one can get any more time. Because everybody has exactly the same amount of time, the emphasis in time management must be focused on making the best use of the time that you have. The literature contains a massive amount of information on time management. Many of the books and articles have their own unique approach to time management. Most of the materials, however, contain the same core principles.

The key principles for managing time effectively are summarized below.

1. Determine the things that have to be done. Include everything that is important, including ensuring time for family, leisure activities, and rest.
2. Classify the things that have to be done into three or four groups based on their priority. Then complete the list of activities with the highest priority before attempting to do things in the lower priority groups.
3. Handle paper only once. Going through documents, putting them on the desk, and going back to them later requires more effort and time than finishing with the documents the first time you work with them.
4. Be organized. Disorganization wastes a tremendous amount of time. Time spent looking for things could be spent accomplishing the task instead.
5. Keep a schedule. Determine how much time an activity (including meetings) should have and stick to the schedule. Procrastinating destroys schedules. It is also important to be mindful of other people's schedules as well.

Good time management is important. It ensures that we do the important things first and that we plan time for all things that are truly important to us.

ms

Application 8C-5

Heritage Productions, Inc.

Heritage Productions

TO: Mr. Gregory Garrison

FROM: HRM Team

DATE: Current date

SUBJECT: Characteristics of an Effective Team

Based on our experiences working in teams, the HRM team compiled a list of characteristics that we felt were important characteristics of an effective team. In addition, we used the Internet and our library to research the literature on effective teams. The characteristics gleaned from the literature were added to our list.

Each characteristic was discussed, and the team ranked the characteristics in order of priority for an effective team. The ten characteristics that the team determined to be the most important characteristics of an effective team are summarized below.

Characteristics of an Effective Team

1. All team members clearly understand the goals that the team is trying to accomplish and should have the ability to contribute to achieving those goals.
2. All team members place the goals of the team above their own personal goals and are willing to do what is necessary to achieve team goals.
3. All team members play an active role in determining the ways in which team goals can best be accomplished.
4. All team members recognize and understand the roles they must play in order for the team to accomplish its goals.
5. All team members meet their commitments and are willing to do their fair share of the work and even a little more when it is necessary to meet team goals.
6. All team members actively participate in making decisions that affect the team.
7. All team members support team decisions—regardless of their original positions on the issue—once the decisions have been made.
8. Every team member respects every other team member regardless of the role the team member plays.
9. All team members share in both the successes and the failures of the team.
10. All team members should feel comfortable as members of the team and should have "team spirit."

We believe that a team that truly possess all of these characteristics will be an effective team.

Application 8E

GOODWILL AND PERSONAL BUSINESS MESSAGES

9

Chapter 9 was added to this edition specifically to get students to focus on the importance of building good relationships in business. Personal business messages help to build goodwill and to strengthen relationships. Point out to students the importance of sincerity in personal business messages. If you genuinely care about your business associates, you will want to share in their happy occasions and to show concern when misfortune happens.

Customers like to do business with people who are warm, friendly, and trustworthy. Personal business messages help to demonstrate these qualities. The letters that are illustrated use a very straightforward approach that is similar to good news messages. The topic of the thank you note illustrated was selected specifically to lay the groundwork for the next chapter on employment communications. Fewer than 50 percent of people granted an interview write a thank you note. They miss a great opportunity to demonstrate the good personal communication skills that companies value.

Review Guide 7: Use Concrete Language (Page 191)

APPLICATION 9A

1. Marjorie will send a $1,000 donation to the symphony on May 1.

2. You need to get a size XXL sweatshirt for Bill because he is 6'4" and weighs 240 pounds.

3. Pat put $50,000 in the savings account and earned 8 percent interest

4. The team won eight games by less than 3 points each.

5. A thousand fans drove 600 miles to watch the No. 2 team lose to the No. 15 team.

APPLICATION 9B — *Editing and Language Arts Checkpoint (Page 192)*

Refer to page 111 of Appendix B for the solution keyed to the language arts guides.

**PPLICATION 9C** — *Writing Personal Business and Goodwill Messages (Pages 194–195)*

Sample solutions for the six documents are on pages 88–91. Emphasize to students the importance of good human relations skills. Point out that personal documents must be sincere, warm, and friendly or they will not achieve their objective. Encourage students to get in the habit of writing these goodwill building messages promptly.

The documents are sent to a variety of industries so that students will understand that personal business messages are appropriate in all types of settings. Industries include

- manufacturing
- medical supplies
- office furniture
- service

Student solutions will vary.

PPLICATION 9D — *Self-Assessment (Pages 196–197)*

1. Short Answer

   a. It is important to write personal business messages because they build goodwill and help to establish good relationships with customers, employees, or other business associates. In many cases, it is a matter of good manners to say thank you for things done for you.

   b. Congratulatory notes are written to celebrate successes of businesses or individuals, such as when they win awards, get promotions, or expand business. Thank you notes are written to show appreciation after someone has done something for you, such as interviewing you, taking you out for a meal, or give you business or a gift. Special occasion messages are written to commemorate special events in the lives of associates or businesses, such as an anniversary or special holiday.

   c. E-mail would be appropriate for congratulatory messages that you want to share with a large distribution list, such as all employees. E-mail is generally used for internal messages rather than external messages.

   d. Congratulatory messages are written in a straightforward, sincere way. The tone should be warm and friendly. The messages should be short. The strategy is similar to a good news message.

   e. Technology facilitates personal business messages by making special fonts (such as script) and clip art available. E-mail is also used internally for some personal business messages.

2. See sample solution 9D-2 on page 92.

CASE STUDY

Heritage Productions (Page 198)

Students' answers may vary widely for this exercise. Depending on the country selected, the holidays and the customs will be different. Point out to students that keywords: *country name plus holidays* should produce information needed. Note that some holidays are fixed; other holidays vary from year to year. Therefore, point out to the students the importance of keeping the information current. Customs will vary widely. The key to building relationships is to gain a better understanding of the culture of the country in which you do business. The more you know about the culture, the more you can relate appropriately to your business associates.

Viking Manufacturing Company

220 E. 40th Street
Holland, MI 49422-0802
(616) 555-0165

Current date

Ms. Marjorie Ducate
Chief Executive Officer
GreenGate Industries
1283 Greystone Road
Waterbury, CT 06704-2248

Dear Ms. Ducate

Congratulations! GreenGate Industries is most deserving of the National Manufacturing Quality Award, and we are delighted that you received this highly coveted award. To be one of the top five manufacturing companies nationally is a major achievement.

We are proud to be a supplier of GreenGate, and we were delighted that we had the opportunity to provide information for the award process. The emphasis you place on quality is evident in all your dealings with us.

Again, congratulations on achieving this outstanding award.

Sincerely

Student's Name

ms

Application 9C–1

Western Community College

Business Department ■ 1837 West Avenue
Durham, NC 27704-6208

The Mustangs

Current date

Mr. Martin Rickenhouser
Marketing Manager
Diamond Modular Office Systems
7849 Highway 751
Durham, NC 27713-9032

Dear Mr. Rickenhouser

The day our class spent at Diamond Modular Office Systems was both very educational and very enjoyable. The tour of your manufacturing plant and your showrooms gave us an opportunity to see the latest in office furniture and layout as well as an understanding of how the modular systems were manufactured.

The presentation by your designer, Ms. Leigh James, was very interesting and supplemented what we learned in class. Ms. James provided us with many new ideas that will be useful in the office layouts that we must design.

The class also enjoyed and appreciated the delicious lunch that you provided. Lunch in your employee dining area was a special treat for all of us.

On behalf of our entire Office Management class, thank you again, Mr. Rickenhouser, for hosting an excellent field trip. We learned a great deal and appreciate your serving as our host.

Sincerely

Student's Name

ms

Application 9C–2

VanHuss Industries, Inc.

TO: All Employees

FROM: Student's Name

DATE: Current date

SUBJECT: Award for Roxanne Merriwether

Please join me in congratulating Roxanne Merriwether, an accountant in the Administration Division of VanHuss Industries. Roxanne received the Community Volunteer Award. This award is given to the one citizen each year who has made the most outstanding contribution to the community.

Roxanne richly deserves this honor. As many of you may know, she is active in the United Way, Junior Achievement, the Better Business Bureau, the Chamber of Commerce, and several charitable groups. We are extremely proud of Roxanne and appreciate very much her contributions to the community.

VanHuss Industries is extremely pleased to have one of its employees who is so active in our community be recognized in this outstanding manner.

ms

Application 9C–3

VanHuss Industries, Inc.

TO: All Employees

FROM: Student's Name

DATE: Current date

SUBJECT: Annual Picnic

The VanHuss Industries annual picnic for all employees is scheduled on June 15 from Noon to 8 p.m. at the Lakefront Club. Your families or guests are cordially invited to join in the fun.

Food, beverages, and a wide variety of recreational activities will be provided. Put on your comfortable, casual attire and join your colleagues for fun and fellowship.

We look forward to another relaxing day with you and your family or guest.

Application 9C–4A

υ b c

VanHuss Industries
Annual Picnic

June 15

Noon to 8 p.m.

Lakefront Club

Beverages   Recreational Activities   Food

Bring your family or guest and join in the fun

Very Casual

Application 9C–4B

VanHuss Industries, Inc.

TO: Doug Smith, Maintenance Supervisor

FROM: Student's Name, Manager of Human Resources

DATE: Current date

SUBJECT: Best Wishes—25th Anniversary

Best wishes to you, Doug, as you celebrate your 25th anniversary with VanHuss Industries on Monday. This event represents a major milestone in your career, and I am delighted to have been a colleague of yours for many of those years.

You will, of course, be formally recognized at the annual meeting at the end of the year when all anniversaries are celebrated. However, I wanted to share with you my very best wishes on the day of your anniversary.

We appreciate the many contributions you have made to VanHuss Industries during the past 25 years, and we wish you continued success in your career.

ms

Application 9C–6

Student's Name

Your Street Address
City, State, Postal Code

Current date

Dr. Marshall Burge, Ph.D.
Professor, Business Administration
Central State University
Chattanooga, TN 37406-4829

Dear Dr. Burge

Thank you very much for providing me with an excellent recommendation for a summer position at Baytown Medical Supplies. I have accepted a position as an office assistant, and I think that I will enjoy the experience and learn a great deal from it.

Your letter was instrumental in my obtaining this position, and I appreciate your taking the time to write a letter on my behalf. I look forward to sharing my summer experiences with you when I return to Central in the fall.

Sincerely

Student's Name

ms

Application 9C–5

VanHuss Industries, Inc.

TO: Mr. Carl G. Wentworth, Benefits Manager

FROM: Student's Name

DATE: Current date

SUBJECT: Best Wishes for Your Retirement

Please accept my very best wishes for a long and happy retirement. You certainly deserve to enjoy your retirement after thirty years of outstanding service to VanHuss Industries.

During my two years with the company, you were extremely helpful to me. I especially appreciate the help you gave me when I had surgery and had to miss work for three weeks. Your efforts went far beyond the call of duty.

We will all miss you and the wonderful, close working relationship that we all had with you. Again, I wish you a very enjoyable retirement.

ms

Application 9D–2

Mr. Gregory Garrison
Page 2
Current date

Hierarchy and rank are very important in Germany. Meetings are usually between people of the same rank. You are expected to be well prepared for meetings and to stick to the agenda. Conservative behavior in meetings is expected.

Building Good Relationships

The way to build good relationships is to understand the culture and to demonstrate to your associates that you have made an effort to learn about them and their country. Learning a few words of German such as greetings and commonly used phrases creates a good impression. Try to adapt to the customs of the country you are visiting. Be willing to try the local food and always learn what is appropriate to wear for the particular occasion. Be patient; international friendships take time to develop.

Please let us know if you need additional information.

ms

Application 9E

Heritage Productions, Inc.

Heritage Productions

TO: Mr. Gregory Garrison

FROM: HRM Team

DATE: Current date

SUBJECT: Research on Holidays and Customs of Germany

The information you requested about Germany follows.

Holidays

In Germany, some holidays are fixed and others vary year by year. Also, some regions celebrate holidays that other regions do not. The following is a general list of German holidays:

- January 1 — New Year's Day
- January 6 — Epiphany (regional)
- Easter (varies)
- Ascension Thursday (40 days after Easter)
- May 1 — May Day (Labor Day)
- Whitmonday (50 days after Easter)
- Corpus Christi (60 days after Easter—regional)
- August 15 — Assumption (regional)
- October 3 — German Unity Day
- November 1 — All Saints Day (regional)
- Day of Prayer and Repentance (Third Wednesday in November)
- December 25 — Christmas (plus day before and day after if on workday)

Customs of Doing Business

Germans tend to be rather formal; therefore, use titles unless you have already established a very good relationship with your associates. Germans tend to be precise and use statistics and documentation for credibility. You should be prepared to back up statements you make. They also expect business appointments to be conducted as scheduled. Being late is not appreciated.

Application 9E

EMPLOYMENT COMMUNICATIONS

Chapter 10 will be of special interest to many students because they are looking for either a part-time or a full-time job. This chapter is not dependent on other chapters and can be taught at any time that it is needed by students. If this chapter is taught out of sequence, students can be referred to Chapter 5 on persuasive writing and to the thank you for an interview note illustrated in Chapter 9.

Students are introduced to the employment process from both the employer and the employee perspective. However, the assignments they are asked to write focus on the communication skills they will need to know once they are in the job market. At this stage in their careers and in a basic text, students need to focus on selling themselves effectively.

DEVELOPING AN EMPLOYMENT STRATEGY

The self-analysis process is a critical but painful process required before an effective résumé or letter of application can be written. Students need to be aware that getting a job requires meeting the needs of the employer. The earlier in the education process that students understand this, the more able they are to tailor their education to meet their career objectives.

Students also need to understand that rarely do other people "get" jobs for them, nor do jobs just fall into their laps. Finding a job is one of the most important things they will do. Finding the right job takes hard work, persistence, and carefully directed efforts. Networking may be the most important factor in getting a foot in the door.

APPLICANT TRACKING SYSTEMS

The employment process is becoming automated in many companies. Most people think of automated systems for employment in large companies, and most large companies do use automated systems for tracking applicants. The surprise to many people is that the employment process in smaller companies is affected as well. The primary reason is that many small companies outsource the human resources function. The companies that provide the human resources services to smaller businesses can do so economically because they are highly automated.

The résumés illustrated in this text are a blend between electronic résumés and traditional résumés. They include enough nouns to show up in keyword searches, but they also appeal to the decision makers who will read them once they pass the computer screening. The following process is used by many companies that use applicant tracking systems.

- The person responsible for the vacant position indicates keywords for required qualifications. For example, an associate degree may be required. Keywords might be *associate degree, AA degree,* or *AS degree.* For a position that requires word processing, the keywords might be the name of the software package the company uses.
- The desirable qualifications are listed next by keywords. Keywords might include *communication skills, words a minute* for keyboarding rates, and *organization skills.*
- The computer searches first for **required** keywords and then for **desired** keywords. If required keywords are not present, the application is not selected from the database.
- Applications that have the required keywords are selected and scanned for desirable qualifications. The computer selects the applications that have all required qualifications and some desired qualifications.
- The applications are referred to the individuals who review them to determine which applicants should be invited for an interview.

Graphics, vertical lines, and other items that decorate or clutter résumés do not scan well. Therefore, students should be cautioned about using them on résumés. Black type on white paper works best. Most scanners can handle bold type. Sans serif fonts are preferred over serif fonts.

Typically, student résumés should be written concisely and should fit on one page. Individuals with more experience may have longer résumés. Appearance makes a difference. Careful editing and proofreading are critical.

Review Guide 8: Use Effective Sentence and Paragraph Structure (Page 215)

APPLICATION 10A

1. Please place the plant near the window in the waiting room.

2. If your arm has a cast on it, the cast will be removed in approximately six weeks.

3. Pat likes shopping in expensive stores, finding good bargains, and decorating the house with those purchases.

   or

   Pat likes to shop in expensive stores, to find good bargains, and to decorate the house with those purchases.

4. Answers will vary widely.

5. Answers will vary widely.

Editing and Language Arts Checkpoint (Pages 216–217)

APPLICATION 10B

Refer to page 112 of Appendix B for the solution keyed to the language arts guides.

APPLICATION 10C
Writing Employment Messages (Pages 218–219)

The industries represented will vary widely depending on the job interests of the students. The solutions will also vary dramatically. The two résumés and three job application letters illustrated in the textbook can be used as sample solutions for all the exercises.

Time should be spent talking about how to present strengths and weaknesses to an employer. Students usually can identify their strengths and discuss them reasonably well. Help needs to be given for weaknesses. Teach students how to present a weakness and try to turn it into a strength. For example,

A weakness is that I tend to procrastinate on doing work. However, I have been working on time management and find that by setting priorities and doing jobs in order of priority, I have improved my time management significantly.

APPLICATION 10D
Self-Assessment (Pages 220–221)

1. Short Answer

   a. The hidden job market can be tapped through networking. Talking to people knowledgeable in the field, reading journals read by people in the field, talking to instructors and to a wide range of contacts are the best ways to find out about jobs.

   b. An applicant tracking system is an electronic way of maintaining information about job applicants. Information about applicants is stored in a database and scanned for a match when a position is available.

   c. Traditional résumés usually are written in an action-oriented way. Action or power verbs are used extensively. Electronic résumés place more emphasis on including nouns to match keyword searches.

   d. The most important thing to consider is which style will present your strengths in the best way. If you have a lot of experience, a reverse chronological order résumé builds on your experience. If you have very little experience, a functional résumé that shows knowledge, skill, and potential would be to your advantage.

   e. The following strategy usually works well for employment letters.

   - Establish a point of contact.
   - Specify the type of job you seek.
   - Highlight your qualifications.
   - Refer to enclosed résumé.
   - Request an interview.

2. Letters will vary widely depending on the ad selected and the qualifications of the students.

C A S E S T U D Y   APPLICATION 10E

Heritage Productions (Page 222)

Students' answers may vary widely for this exercise depending on what they happened to find surfing the Internet. Suggest to students that they try to find something on a particular country and a particular company. That way they will get a sample of information that other companies in the country of interest are using to distribute job information. Typically, the answers should indicate that Heritage can use the Internet in other countries in almost the same way they do domestically.

Most students will suggest that Heritage could have a web page with a page on employment and links to specific employment available in the countries. The Internet can also be used to find information on the various work permits required of noncitizens in various countries.

Editing and Language Arts Checkpoint Guides

Cluster	Description
C	**Capitalization Cluster**
C.1	Capitalize nouns which identify persons, places, things, or trade names, and the pronoun *I*; do not capitalize common nouns.
C.2	Capitalize the first word of a sentence; also capitalize the first word of complete sentences in quotation marks or following a colon.
C.3	Capitalize days of the week, months of the year, and holidays.
C.4	Capitalize titles within an address and those that precede a proper name; generally do not capitalize job titles that stand alone or that follow a name unless they are titles of extreme distinction.
C.5	Capitalize specific department, board, committee, or division names; do not capitalize organizational terms that stand alone.
C.6	Capitalize names of geographic regions or districts; do not capitalize compass directions or general locations.
C.7	Capitalize specific course names and main words in titles of articles and books; do not capitalize general course names.
C.8	Capitalize nouns which precede numbers and letters except page, paragraph, and line references.
G	**Grammar Usage Cluster**
G.1	**Grammar usage—subjects/verbs**
G.1-1	Use complete sentences; i.e., sentences with both a subject and a verb.
G.1-2	Ensure that subjects and verbs agree in person and number; use nouns and objects appropriately.
G.1-3	Use the appropriate tense of a verb to express time.
G.2	**Grammar usage—pronouns**
G.2-1	Ensure that a pronoun agrees with its antecedent in person, number, and gender.
G.2-2	Use the nominative case of pronouns for subject and predicate nouns, the objective case as direct and indirect objects, the possessive case to denote ownership.
G.2-3	Who, whom, which, and that are often confusing. Use who and whom to refer to people. Use who as the subject of a verb; use whom as the object of a verb. Use which and that to refer to things. Use that in restrictive clauses (provide essential information); use which in nonrestrictive clauses (provide additional non-essential information).
G.3	**Grammar usage—adjectives**
G.3-1	Use adjectives to modify nouns or pronouns.
G.3-2	Use positive degree of comparison for equal or no comparison; use comparative degree for comparison of two unequal items; use superlative degree for comparison of three or more items.
G.4	**Adverbs**
G.4-1	Use adverbs to modify verbs, adjectives, and other adverbs.
G.4-2	Use appropriate comparison for adverbs.
G.5	**Grammar usage—prepositions and conjunctions**

Cluster	Description
G.5-1	Use conjunctions appropriately to show connecting relationships.
G.5-2	Use prepositions appropriately to show the relationship between a noun or pronoun and other words in a sentence.
G.6	**Grammar usage—possessives**
G.6-1	Use apostrophe s to form possessive of singular and plural nouns not ending in s.
G.6-2	Use apostrophe to form possessive of plural nouns ending in s.
G.6-3	Use possessive pronouns appropriately.
G.6-4	Add apostrophes to the last owner's name to show joint ownership; use apostrophe s to each owner's name to show separate ownership.
N	**Number Usage For Business Writing Cluster**
N.1	**Number Usage—general conventions**
N.1-1	Spell out numbers one to ten; use numerals for numbers larger than ten.
N.1-2	Spell out numbers that begin sentences.
N.1-3	Use words for approximate or large round numbers (1-2 words); use numbers for round numbers in millions or higher with word modifier.
N.1-4	When two numbers are adjacent, use figures for one and words for the other.
N.1-5	Use figures for page numbers.
N.1-6	Use figures for units of measure and with symbols.
N.2	**Number Usage—dates and time**
N.2-1	Use figures with a.m. and p.m.; use words with o'clock.
N.2-2	Use figures for days following months; use ordinals (th, d, st) only when number precedes the month or is used alone.
N.3	**Number Usage—percentages, fractions, money**
N.3-1	Use figures with percentages (except infrequent use in text if 1-2 words).
N.3-2	Use figures when expressing money.
N.3-3	Do not add zeros to even sums of money; add zeros for mixed sums; do not write numbers in figures then in words except for legal use.
N.3-4	Spell out fractions unless they are in a combination with whole numbers.
N.4	**Number Usage—addresses**
N.4-1	Use words for street names one to ten; figures for numbers above ten.
N.4-2	Use figures for highways.
N.4-3	Use figures for house numbers and post office boxes except for the number one.
P	**Punctuation Cluster**
P.1	**Punctuation—comma**

Cluster	Description
P.1-1	Use a comma to set off introductory words, long introductory phrases, and introductory dependent clauses.
P.1-2	Use a comma to set off independent clauses joined by a coordinating conjunction; do not use a comma to separate a compound verb
P.1-3	Use a comma to separate three or more items in a series (the comma before a conjunction is optional)
P.1-4	Use a comma to set off a nonrestrictive clause or phrase; do not use a comma with a restrictive clause or phrase.
P.1-5	Use a comma to set off nonessential or interrupting elements in a sentence.
P.1-6	Use a comma to set off words of direct address.
P.1-7	Use a comma to separate the day from the year or date and the city from the state.
P.1-8	Use a comma to introduce a quotation.
P.1-9	Use a comma to set off contrasting phrases and clauses and for transitional words.
P.1-10	Use a comma to set off two or more parallel adjectives (*and* could substitute for the comma).
P.2	**Punctuation—colon, semicolon**
P.2-1	Use a colon to introduce enumerations, lists, or a long, formal quote and between hours, minutes, and seconds when figures are used.
P.2-2	Use a semicolon to separate independent clauses when the conjunction is omitted.
P.2-3	Use a semicolon to separate independent clauses linked by conjunctive adverbs, transitional words, or phrases.
P.2-4	Use a semicolon between items in a series when the items contain commas.
P.3	**Punctuation—period, question mark, exclamation point**
P.3-1	Use a period after a complete sentence, indirect question, or courteous request.
P.3-2	Use a question mark after a direct question or a series of questions.
P.3-3	Use an exclamation point after emotional words, phrases, or exclamatory statements.
P.4	**Punctuation—hyphen, apostrophe, quotation marks**
P.4-1	Use a hyphen to join a compound adjective that forms a single unit preceding the noun it modifies; do not use a hyphen if the first word is an adverb ending in *ly*.
P.4-2	Use a hyphen to join compound numbers between 21 and 99 and fractions when they are spelled out and used as a modifier.
P.4-3	Use a hyphen with the prefixes *ex*, *self*, and between a prefix and a capitalized word.
P.4-4	Use an apostrophe with contractions, to show omissions, and as a symbol for feet and minutes.
P.4-5	Use quotation marks to enclose titles and direct quotations; long quotations that are indented do not require quotation marks.
T	**Titles of Works**
T.1	Italicize title of books, newspapers, magazines, movies, and plays.
T.2	Put quotation marks around parts of a larger work, such as the title of an article or column in a newspaper.
T.3	Put quotation marks around titles of radio and television shows.

Cluster	Description	
W	**Word Usage / Spell Check Challenge Cluster**	
W.1	a	article used before words beginning with a consonant
	an	article used before words beginning with a vowel
W.2	accept	(v.) receive or take; agree to
	except	(prep.) leave out; other than; (v.) omit; exclude
W.3	advice	(n.) recommendation
	advise	(v.) give counsel
W.4	affect	(v.) change or influence
	effect	(n.) outcome or result; (n.) to cause or bring about
W.5	appraise	(v.) establish value
	apprise	(v.) notify or inform
W.6	capital	(n.) wealth or net worth; city that is seat of government
	capitol	(n.) chief building of a government; state house
W.7	cite	(v.) quote or summon
	sight	(n.) vision; worth seeing
	site	(n.) location or place
W.8	coarse	(adj.) rough texture or finish
	course	(n.) line of motion; series of lectures; place to play golf; method
W.9	complement	(v.) to complete or fill
	compliment	(n.) praise; present with gift
W.10	council	(n.) an appointed or elected group of advisers
	counsel	(n.) advice; (v.) advise
W.11	eminent	(adj.) distinguished; famous
	imminent	(adj.) threatening; about to happen
W.12	form	(n.) shape, standard document
	from	(prep.) separation; away
W.13	knew	(v.) past tense of know
	new	(adj.) recently made; unused
W.14	loose	(adj.) not restrained or secured
	lose	(v.) suffer a loss; not know where to find
W.15	peace	(n.) calm; tranquil
	piece	(n.) portion of; quantity
W.16	personal	(adj.) private; individual
	personnel	(n.) staff; employees
W.17	exceed	(vb.) go beyond
	precede	(v.t.) come before
	proceed	(v.i.) continue; go forward
W.18	principal	(adj. or n.) head of school; main; chief; sum of money
	principle	(n.) basic truth; rule of conduct
W.19	quiet	(adj.) still; noiseless
	quite	(adv.) completely; very
W.20	stationary	(adj.) fixed; not moving
	stationery	(n.) writing paper
W.21	perspective	(n.) mental view
	prospective	(adj.) likely to happen
W.22	access	(n.) able to obtain or make use of
	excess	(adj.) more than the usual or specified

Application 2B—Solution Document

TO: Department Managers

FROM: Your Name

DATE: May 20, 19—

SUBJECT: Technology Changes

The **Executive Committee** plans to **meet** on **Tuesday**, June **6**, 1997, at **two**
C.5   G.1-3   C.3   P.1-7   N.2-1
o'clock to develop a strategic plan for implementing technology changes. At **its** meeting
G.6-3
last **March 15**, the **members** of the committee discussed our current technology status
N.2-2   C.1
with Ashley **Price**, a leading **consultant** with Central Technology **Services**, and asked for
P.1-5   C.4   C.1
her **advice**. **She** agreed to **appraise** our **situation and** to report back to us.
W.3   G.2-2   W.5   P.1-2
Ashley called **Rick**, our **personnel** manager, this **past** week and **said, "May I**
P.1-5   W.16   G.3-2   P.1-8   C.2
interview **five managers** and about **twenty experienced**, knowledgeable computer **users?**
N.1-1 C.4   N.1-3   P.1-10   P.3-2
If it is possible, Rick, please schedule the interviews during the **first part of next **week."**
N.1-1   P.4-5
Rick **is** scheduling **three-fourths** hour slots for **managers'** interviews **and a half-hour**
G.1-2   N.3-4   G.6-2   W.1   P.4-2
slot for each computer **users** interview. All managers should do **their** best to
G.6-1   G.2-1
accommodate **this request** (or **these requests**) **from** Rick for staff and managerial time.
G.2-1   W.12
If you are unable to schedule an interview early next **week**, please call me **immediately**
P.1-1   G.4-1
so that I can **choose** someone else **who** can participate.
G.1-2   G.2-3
Please report **to Conference Room A** in our **new** facility on Highway **10** on the
G.5-2 C.8   W.13   N.4-2
south side of town for your interview. This **site** is **more** convenient for staff than the
C.6   W.7 G.4-2
building at **One Main Street**, and it is very **quiet**. **Reminder!** Allow 15 minutes to get
N.4-3   P.1-2   W.19   P.3-3
there in plenty of time for your interview. **Also**, please read the 12-page report that is
G.4-1   P.1-1
attached. The information on **page 5** about our mainframe **computer will be of**
C.8   N.1-5   G.1-1
(**computer may be of**, or **computer is of**) particular interest.   ⟶

As our **consultant** points out in the report, personal **computers, not mainframe**
C.4   P.1-9
computers, are the wave of the future. About **75 percent** of our computing is handled by
P.1-9   N.3-1
our mainframe. **Two hundred** personal computers handle the other **25 percent** of our
N.1-2   N.3-1
computing. Of the **200, fifty** (or **of the two-hundred, 50**) are 386 processors. Our
N.1-4
consultant **counsels** us that the **computers with 386 processors** need to be replaced at
W.10   P.1-4
one time rather **than** in a **piecemeal** fashion. We also need to install **a network, upgrade**
G.5-1   W.15   P.1-3
software, and add (or **upgrade software and add**) more storage capability. If we

accept our **consultant's advice,** our **Long-Range** Budget **Committee** will, of **course,**
W.2   G.6-1   W.3   P.4-1   C-5   W.8
have to determine the **effect** replacing **these** computers will have on our **capital** budget
W.4   G.2-1   W.6
before we **proceed** with this action.
W.17
   The predicted cost is **$2 million which** is **significantly higher** than our current
C.2   N.1-3   G.2-3   P.4-1
budget for computer hardware and **software; consequently,** we will have to act very
P.2-3   P.1-9
cautiously. I estimate it will cost **$2,400** to replace each 386 **computer; the** (or
G.4-2   N.3-3   P.2-2
computer. The) software will be an additional **$500.** We only owe **$5,000** on the
N.3-2   N.3-3
principal of the loan on the mainframe **computer;** therefore, we will probably keep it.
W.18   P.2-2
   It's imminent that our technology will be **upgraded; we** (or **upgraded. We**)
P.4-4 W.11   P.2-2
must **complement** our investment in hardware with an investment in our **personnel.** We
W.9   W.16
have explored both **self-paced** training and the new course, **Arntson Computer-Based**
P.4-3   C.7
Training for Windows. We will report on all of these developments at the **June** meeting.
C.3

Application 3B—Solution Document

TO: Jan Marks, Training Manager

FROM: Student's Name

DATE: June 8, 19—

SUBJECT: Effective Team Building Training Materials

Thank you for giving me **an** opprtunity to review the *Effective Team Building* training
         W.1
materials. I **examined** the training package **from** both the **perspective** of the trainer and our
         G.1-3   W.12   W.21
personnel who would take the **course.** I also tried to **appraise** the value relative to **its** cost.
W.16   W.8   W.5   G.6
From the **trainer's** perspective, the materials **are** comprehensive. The package **includes**
            G.6-1   G.1-2   G.1-2
an **outline,** a trainee manual, audio and video **tapes,** slides, and an assessment. The content is
    P.1-3   P.1-3
relevant and is **written** in a **clear,** concise way. Very little reinforcement is **provided, however**.
         G.1-3   P.1-10   P.1-9
From the **learner's** perspective, the material has only one major **flaw.** The learner is not
            G.6-1   G.2-1
required to participate **actively.** Overall **though,** the program is **quite** good.
                  G.4-1   P.1-1   W.19
The complete program with materials for **75** trainees is **priced** at **$6,000** or about **$80**
                              N.1-1   G.1-3   N.3-3   N.3-2
per trainee. Additional training packets are **$60 each,** which will make the per employee cost
                              N.3-2 P.1-4
slightly lower if we train all **those** employees **who** work in a team environment. This program
G.4-1   G.2-2   G.2-3
is the **most** expensive of the **three** programs that we have evaluated. These costs do **not, of**
      G.3-2   N.1-1   P.1-5
course, include the time of our employees.
   P.1-5
Since one additional training program is scheduled to arrive for review on June **15,** I
                                                                              N.2-2
recommend that the decision be **postponed** to see if that program is more cost **effective than**
                        G.1-3   W.4   G.5-1
this one. I plan to be at the Highway **12** Training Center on the **16th** of **June,** and I will be
                              N.4-2   N.2-2   P.1-2
happy to review the materials while I am **there** if you would like me to do so.
                                    G.4-1

Application 4B—Solution Document

The Board of Directors of the Economic Alliance **has** scheduled a meeting with Robert
<small>C.2</small> <small>G.1-2</small>
West, Mayor of Horrell **Hill;** Judy Ledbetter, President of County **Council;** and Wayne
<small>P.2-4</small> <small>W.10</small> <small>P.2-4</small>
Roxbury, Secretary of **Commerce;** at **1:45** on **Tuesday,** March 26. The primary purpose of the
<small>P.1-4</small> <small>P.2-4 P.2-1</small> <small>P.1-7</small>
meeting is to identify two **pieces** of land **north** of Highway **10** that have **100** acres per **site** and
<small>W.15</small> <small>C.6</small> <small>N.4-2</small> <small>N.1-6</small> <small>W.7</small>
take **initial** steps to obtain options to purchase this land. **This** step is critical so that we will not
<small>G.3-1</small> <small>G.1-2</small>
lose out on economic development prospects again because of our inability to locate suitable
<small>W.14</small>
sites for manufacturing plants immediately.
<small>W.7</small>

The Economic Alliance will also review Bob **Smith and Tom Graham's** proposal to
<small>G.6-4</small>
upgrade the conference room and shift **from** portable projection equipment to a **stationary**
<small>W.12</small> <small>W.20</small>
multimedia platform for presentations to visiting prospects. The funds are available for the

project; permission is **needed** to build a base platform that is **12** feet long, **6** feet deep, and
<small>P.2-2</small> <small>G.1-3</small> <small>N.1-6</small> <small>N.1-6</small>
10 inches high. The multimedia podium will be mounted on this base platform.
<small>N.1-6</small>

The last item **proposed** is a plan to beautify Rosewood Boulevard between **First** Street
<small>G.4-2</small> <small>N.4-1</small>
and **Ninth** Street. This area is the gateway to our city and **needs** to be enhanced with
<small>N.4-1</small> <small>G.1-2</small>
landscaping, benches, and appropriate lighting to create a positive first impression for visitors

to the city. The landscape architect with **whom** we have consulted has provided a cost estimate
<small>G.2-3</small>
for the project. **An** architectural drawing of the area will be on display at the meeting.
<small>W.1 and C.2</small> <small>P.1-1</small>
The Board **welcomes** your comments or suggestions on these topics prior to the
<small>G.1-2</small>
meeting. Please send them to me as early as possible.

Application 5B—Solution Document

Thank you for giving me the opportunity to review the Productivity Improvement and Cost Reduction proposal **Christopher** McBride **submitted** to you and to give my assessment of
C.1   G.1-3
it. I analyzed the proposal **carefully,** and I have a number of **reservations** about it even though
G.4-2   P.1-2   G.1-2
Christopher McBride is an **eminent** consultant.
W.11

My **principal** concern is that the approach Christopher proposed is **a** standard industrial
W.18   W.1
engineering approach. **Its** major emphasis is on efficiency rather than on **effectiveness.** The
G.6-3   W.4
industrial engineering approach works reasonably **well** for some factory and routine clerical
G.4-1
operations; however, it generally does not produce good results in a work setting involving
P.2-3   P.1-9
professionals. My second concern **is** the cost quoted. The first phase cost of **$25,000** is about
G.1-2   N.3-3
20 percent too high.
N.3-1   G.4-1

As we discussed earlier, most of your **personnel** are professional employees—many of
W.16
whom are doing routine work that could be **delegated** to support staff. Delegating **effectively**
G.2-3   G.1-3   W.4
would reduce **costs** and enhance the positions of your support staff **substantially. Christopher's**
G.6-1   G.4-1   G.6-1
proposal **does** not address this issue at all.
G.1-2

My **advice** to you is to try to obtain a proposal that **focuses** on effectiveness and that is
W.3   G.1-2
designed for professional employees. I have a meeting in your building on **Monday, March 14,**
C.3   P.1-7   P.1-7
from 2:15 to 3:15 in **Conference Room C** and could meet with you about the proposal at 3:30.
W.12   P.2-1   P.2-1   C.1
Just **let** me know if you want to meet at that time.
G.1-2

Application 6B—Solution Document

Data from the Outsourcing Printing Report clearly showed that the cost of printing could be reduced **substantially** by discontinuing the outsourcing of many of VanHuss Industries
G.4-1
printing jobs. Therefore, a **second** phase of the report **was authorized** to determine the
N.1-1   G.1-2 G.1-3
feasibility of setting up an in-house electronic publishing system.

Problem

The primary purpose of **this** phase of the project **was** to determine the percentage and type of
G.2-1   G.1-2
work **that** could be **handled** internally. This information can then be **used** to determine the
G.2-3   G.1-3   G.1-3
best and most cost **effective** system **to** meet the needs of VanHuss Industries.
W.4   G.5-2

Supporting Data

All of the request **forms** for outside printing for the **past** year were collected and analyzed
W.12   G.4-1
to determine the type and volume of printing. In many cases, job samples **had** to be obtained
G.1-3
and were analyzed by the printing production team **who** determined whether or not the job
G.2-3
could be handled internally. Four electronic printing system proposals from local vendors
were analyzed to determine capabilities and prices.

Data Analysis

The **analysis** of the request forms for outside printing showed that during the past year about
G.1-2
90 percent of the black and white printing and about **40** percent of the color printing could
N.3-1   N.3-1
have been done **internally** on an electronic publishing **system**. All four of the systems that
G.4-1   G.1-2
were demonstrated to the evaluation team could have handled **those** jobs that were identified
G.1-2   G.2-2
as internal jobs.

All four **systems** include **high-resolution** laser printers with the capability of handling
G.2-1   P.4-1
color as well as black and white copy. The proposals **from** all four vendors **include software,**
W.12   G.1-2   P.1-3
scanners, and two workstations with **two**-page display monitors. The Hess system **uses** two
P.1-3 N.1-1   N.1-1   G.1-2
separate printers—one for color printing and the other for black and white printing. The cost of
the Hess system is **$41,750**. This cost is **$2,000** more **than** the other **systems; however,** the
N.3-3   N.3-2   G.5-1   P.2-3   P.1-9
system **has** advanced features that make it feasible to do additional jobs internally.
G.1-2
Specifications for the four systems and a complete cost analysis are attached.   ⟶

Conclusion

The conclusion of the Outsourcing Printing Report indicated that an in-house system could be justified at a cost of **$80,000** if at least **40** percent of the printing volume could be shifted

N.3-2   N.3-1
internally. The volume of printing that could be shifted internally **far** exceeds the minimum

                                                        G.4-1
requirements, and all systems evaluated meet the cost restrictions. The Hess electronic

P.1-2
publishing system meets the needs of VanHuss Industries **better** than the other three systems.

                                        G.4-2

Recommendation

The Hess system should be purchased and installed within the next **six** weeks. This time frame

                                                N.1-1
allows time **for personnel** in the Printing Center to be adequately trained before the

G.5-2   W.16
outsourcing contract non-renewal notice must be given.

Application 7B—Solution Document

PRESENTATION TO SELECTED STAFF—NOVEMBER 15, 19—

Would you like to have **12** extra hours a week to devote to the responsibilities you think
N.1-1
are the **most** important of everything you do in your **job?** Dr. Ashu **Sopios,** an **eminent expert,**
G.4-2   P.3-2   P.1-4 W.11   P.1-4
completed a communications audit for our company. His conclusion **was** that staff members in the
G.1-2
Business Services Department and the Claims Department could save an average of 12 hours per
C.5
week if the company **developed** an extensive file of **form** documents for situations that **lend**
G.1-3   W.12   G.1-2
themselves to form applications.

As a way of **proceeding** with this task, **Dr.** Sopios suggested that we first identify
W.17   C.4
situations in **which** form letters could be used **effectively**. The **second** step is to determine the
G.2-3   G.4-1   N.1-1
type of form that would be best for each situation. Then form letters can be drafted by a team of

employees **who** are knowledgeable in the area. A **cross-functional** team will review the letters
G.2-2   P.4-1
before approving **them**.
G.2-2
Ten supervisors identified about **fifty** situations in which form letters would save a
N.1-2   N.1-3
significant amount of time. To qualify as a situation requiring a form letter, an average of five

letters a week must be written to customers to solve that situation. Variable forms or form

paragraphs could be used **effectively** in most of the situations. Because complete forms are
W.4
impersonal and guide forms are inefficient, the supervisors recommended that neither complete

forms **nor** guide forms be used.
G.5-1
Supervisors plan to name **five** teams this week to develop the first draft of the form letters.
N.1-1
Each team will be asked to prepare ten form letters. After all letters have been **drafted,** the **cross-**
P.1-1 P.4-1
functional team will review the letters and either approve them or suggest revisions. Employees

who **draft** correspondence in these two areas will be provided with a list and a brief description of
G.1-2
all form letters as well as with a disk containing the form **letters.**
P.3-1

Application 8B—Solution Document

Current date

Dr. Leslie Krisman
4392 Hunter Boulevard S.
Seattle, WA 98144-3847

Dear Dr. Krisman

    The members of the University **Alumni Association who** were present at our annual
_{C.1} _{G.2-3}
meeting truly benefited from **your** outstanding presentation, "Balancing **Life's Demands.**" Many
_{G.6-3} _{G.6-1} _{P.4-5}
members commented **that** the ideas you presented would help all of **us** not only to reduce stress,
_{G.2-1} _{G.2-3} _{G.2-2}
but also to live a fuller and more enriched life. Several members called and **asked** me to print
_{G.1-3}
your presentation in the *Alumni News* so that they could share it with friends and colleagues who
_{T.1}
were not fortunate enough to hear you.
_{G.1-2}
    May we share your ideas with the members of the University **Alumni Association** by
_{C.1}
including a **300**-word abstract of your presentation in the next **issue?** Your article would be
_{G.2-2} _{N.1-1} _{P.3-2}
featured as the lead story with the report of the annual meeting. We would, of **course**, include your
_{W.8}
picture and brief biographical information about you with the article. In order to meet our press

deadlines, we would need to have all information in our office by the **20th** day of this month.
_{P.1-1} _{N.2-2}
    Authors of articles in previous issues of the *Alumni News* have been **quite** pleased with
_{W.19}
the response **they** received **from** the readers. Many reported renewing old friendships and
_{G.2-2} _{W.12}
making new friends. We know our readers would enjoy and benefit from your excellent article.

Yours truly

Student's Name
Editor

ms

Application 9B—Solution Document

TO: Sales Staff

FROM: Student's Name

DATE: Current date

SUBJECT: First Quarter Sales Report

The first quarter revenue figures for **Region IV were** released **today,** and you will be
C.6   G.1-2   P.1-2
pleased to learn that once again the team exceeded **its first** quarter revenue budget.
G.1-3   G.2-2 N.1-1
Congratulations! Each member of the team **exceeded** the individual budget for the first quarter.
P.3-3   W.17
We have **consistently** met both team goals for the **past** three **years,** but rarely has every member
G.4-1   G.1-3   P.1-9
of the team **exceeded** the budget plan. **It's** important that you review carefully the enclosed
G.1-3   P.4-4
report that **itemizes** the revenue generated for all targeted software products.
G.1-2

Of the six application software packages, the one that concerns me **most** is the project
G.4-2
management software. Our project management software sales **are** far below the national average
G.1-2
for the first quarter. In fact, not a single sales representative on our team **met** the budget for
G.1-3
project management software.

Would each of **you** analyze your territory carefully and give me an **account-by-account**
G.2-2   P.4-1
projection of the project management sales for next **quarter?** I have asked Liz **Jordan,** our
P.3-2   P.1-5
technical support **manager,** to come to our next **regularly** scheduled team meeting and talk with
P.1-5   G.4-1
us about ways we can increase our sales in this deficient area. Liz was very instrumental in

helping the **Region III** team increase **its** sales of project management software. I am sure she
C.6   G.2-2
can help us improve our sales in this area.

During the next team **meeting,** we will also view a new product release and begin planning
P.1-1
for launching the sale of this product in our territory. You will be **sent** a product release package
G.1-3
prior to the meeting. Please review it **carefully** so that we can use the meeting time effectively.
G.4-1
Enclosure

Application 10B—Solution Document

Notice—Position Available for Network Manager

Applications for the **newly** created position of network manager **are** now being **accepted** in
G.4-1   G.1-2   W.2
the **Personnel Management Department**. Both internal **and** external applicants must complete the
W.16   C.5   G.5-1
standard application **form**. Forms for internal applicants must contain the signature of the **person's**
W.12   G.6-1
immediate supervisor before they can be **processed**. The deadline for applications **is** June **15**.
G.1-3   G.1-2   N.2-2
The new position is a Grade **12** position in the Administrative Services Division. The new
N.1-1
network manager will report **directly** to the manager of Administrative Services. The **principal**
G.4-1   W.18
reasons this new position was created **were** to provide technical support and training to **users** of
G.1-2   G.1-2
personal computers on the network and **to** have one person who will be totally responsible for
W.16   G.5-2
developing a comprehensive manual for **users** and a network procedures manual. **This** position
G.6-1   G.2-1
requires a person with computer experience as well as knowledge of computer operating systems

and application software. Network knowledge and supervisory experience **are desirable,** but they
G.1-2   P.1-2
are not required. The **new** network manager will be sent to a **three**-week training program in San
W.13   N.1-1
Francisco. The training package was part of the contract for the new network.

The **first** responsibility when the new network manager returns is to develop and offer
N.1-1
training courses for all employees who have **access** to the network at this **site**. The training will
W.22   W.7
complement the other computer training **courses** that are available to employees. The Staff
W.9   W.8
Council advised us to make the courses mandatory for all new network users.
W.10   W.3

PRETEST SOLUTIONS

I. Guides for Writing

1. Please wait until President Hinds arrives before starting the meeting. She should arrive within 10 minutes of the scheduled time.

2. Unless you are familiar with the file, please wait until your supervisor arrives to explain what must be done with it.

3. We appraised the following five houses:

Address	Square Feet	Appraised Value
2934 Louis Lecante Road	5,385	$345,093
8323 Aviation Boulevard	4,750	$276,374
9405 Garners Ferry Road	6,848	$745,500
257 Crown Lake Drive	9,985	$875,000
5234 Braddock Court	4,500	$425,250

4. Please join me for lunch on Friday, October 16, at the Southside Club. I will meet you at 12:15 at the main entrance on Lake Shore Boulevard.

5. President Jones invited us to attend a reception at his home after the game on Saturday.

6. Can we merge the two teams to save as much as possible on meeting expenses?

7. Max and five friends took a three-week African safari that cost $6,500 each.

8. Please put the files on the desk in the office on the lower level.

9. Your payment for your corporate box must arrive before August 1, or the box will be made available to other corporations.

10. Managers should explain their policies on attendance to their employees before enforcing those policies.

II. Short Answer

1. The following steps should be used to plan a message:

   • Determine your objectives and those of the reader.
   • Analyze the reader carefully.

- Make all decisions before writing the memo to determine the best way to present the information.
- Collect all information needed to write the message so that it can be organized effectively.
- Develop the plan for writing, then implement it.

2. The best strategy to use in writing a good-news message is

- present the good news first
- follow up with additional information needed
- close on a warm, friendly note

3. The best strategy to use in writing a negative message is

- begin with a buffer to cushion the bad news
- explain the reasons for the bad news
- present the negative information
- offer alternatives if possible
- close on a positive or, at least, a neutral note

4. A short report contains the following components:

- Identifying information—includes the title, who prepared the report, for whom it was prepared, and the date.
- Problem statement—explains the purpose of the report.
- Supporting data—consists of information collected to solve the problem.
- Data analysis—contains a discussion of the facts and an interpretation of how they can be used to solve the problem.
- Conclusions—describes the results obtained by analyzing and interpreting the facts.
- Recommendations—specifies the course of action that is suggested.
- Summary—consists of a brief synopsis of the report.

5. An electronic résumé is a résumé that has been scanned into a computer system and maintained on-line rather than in paper form. A traditional résumé should be written using action verbs to show results. An electronic résumé should contain nouns that will match the keyword search used for screening electronic résumés. The format should be simple and should avoid vertical lines, clip art, and fonts that do not scan effectively.

VanHuss Industries, Inc.

TO: All Employees

FROM: Student's Name

DATE: Current

SUBJECT: Bone Marrow Screening Drive

Ten minutes of your time may make it possible to extend a child's life for years. Many children, including the son of Martha Louis, an employee in our Shipping Division, suffer from leukemia. In some cases, their only hope is to find a donor whose bone marrow matches theirs.

The County Health Department will be conducting a Bone Marrow Screening Drive at our company next Friday, March 10, from 9:30 a.m. to 3:30 p.m. in the Employee Health Center. The screening procedure is a simple blood test that is not painful. Each donor must also complete a form authorizing the County Health Department to list your donor type in a national registry.

We encourage you to take a few minutes of your time to participate in this worthy cause. A VanHuss Industries employee may be able to give a child the ultimate gift—the hope of life.

pr

Pretest II–2

Palmetto Foundation Selection Committee
Central Carolina University
Gilbert, SC 29054 · (803) 555-0173

Current date

Ms. Angela Martinez
561 Power Point Lane
Lexington, SC 29072

Dear Ms. Martinez

Congratulations! You are the recipient of one of the five $10,000 Palmetto Scholarships awarded each year to outstanding students at Central Carolina University. This scholarship represents outstanding achievement on your part. You were selected from a group of 100 finalists for the scholarship.

This scholarship is renewable each year for four years. To maintain the scholarship you must remain as a full-time student at Central Carolina University and maintain a B or better grade point average.

Again, congratulations on your outstanding achievement. We wish you every success as you pursue your education at Central Carolina University.

Sincerely

Student's name, Chair
Palmetto Foundation Selection Committee

pr

Pretest II–1

TEST SOLUTIONS

1. The cost of communications is influenced by the person producing the document, by the manner in which the document is produced, and by the type of document produced. The salary of the individual creating a document, the time it takes to create and produce that document, and the way that the document is distributed causes the cost of communications to vary significantly. These same factors also affect the quality of communications. For example, the quality of a document depends directly on the communication skills of the writer.

2. Thinking and analytical skills, reading skills, interpersonal skills, information management skills, and the ability to use technology effectively are basic skills that are prerequisite to producing effective written communications.

3. Paying attention to the process of writing is important because processes can be learned. The product or outcome of writing results from using effective processes. Good writing usually involves writing, editing, and revising to achieve desired results. Different approaches for writing can be used. Each writer must select an approach that is comfortable and easy to use.

4. The majority of documents written remain within an organization. Effective communications facilitate the conduct of business. In addition, the documents produced can make either a favorable or a negative impression. Frequently employees are judged by the quality of documents they produce. Upward career mobility often is dependent on the ability to communicate effectively. Internal documents provide an opportunity to showcase communication skills.

5. The mode of communication refers to the method or manner of communicating. Information, for example, can be communicated orally or in writing—using E-mail, the telephone, a written document, or a personal visit. The importance of a document, the sensitivity of the message, the speed required, the need for documentation, the cost, and the destination are examples of factors that influence the mode selection.

6. Writers should carefully examine letters received to gain information about the style preferences of the individual writing the letter as well as to understand the content of the message. Understanding the writer's style provides clues as to the best way to respond to the individual. Good writers pay particular attention to adapting their style to meet the needs of the reader.

7. Examples of technologies that facilitate the creation, production, and distribution of documents are:

- **Application software**—Word processing, spreadsheet, database, and graphics software are useful tools that make it easy to produce high-quality communications.
- **On-line reference tools**—References such as dictionaries, thesauruses, and grammar checkers are useful in improving the quality of documents produced.
- **Laser printers**—These printers produce high quality printing and make it possible to include graphics, color, and other design features.
- **Electronic transmission**—E-mail and fax machines increase the speed at which documents can be distributed.

8. Most companies prefer to distribute documents over an intranet because they can control access to it. Security is a key issue, and most companies do not believe that the Internet provides appropriate levels of security for their proprietary information.

9. People must understand the culture of other countries in which they are doing business in order to deal more effectively with individuals in those countries. Working effectively with individuals in the culture in which you are doing business is likely to produce better results. Understanding the culture helps the writer adapt to the style of the reader.

10. Effective communication is required in virtually every career; therefore, good communication skills are critical for career success. Good communication skills facilitate career growth within an organization and are very marketable to other organizations.

CHAPTER

2

TEST SOLUTIONS

I. Guides for Writing

1. Your application arrived after the directory of participants had been prepared; therefore, it could not be included in the directory.

2. Board meetings should be interrupted only if an emergency situation exists.

3. Please fill out the application and bring it to the receptionist.

4. The program approval process is long and requires approval in the following order:

   • at the department and college levels
   • by the dean
   • by the Committee for Curricula and New Programs
   • by the Faculty Senate or the Graduate Council
   • by the Provost

5. Please consider all the advantages and disadvantages before deciding whether to accept or reject the offer.

6. Brian paid $40 to ensure that the 60-pound package would be delivered within 24 hours.

7. Please water the plants near the door in the foyer.

8. After you called, Martha prepared a new drawing of your landscape design.

9. The company president presented a $10,000 check to the Community Cares Foundation executive director.

10. Contractors must pay express delivery charges if they want their building supplies delivered within 24 hours.

II. Short Answer

1. Passive voice is more effective than active voice when the subject doing the action is irrelevant and when the writer wishes to tone down negative messages.

2. Three factors should be considered carefully in structuring paragraphs:

   • Unity—All ideas in the paragraph relate to one topic.
   • Coherence—Ideas are linked logically to each other.
   • Emphasis—Important ideas are stressed and less important ideas are subordinated.

118

3. The following techniques can be used to emphasize ideas:

- **Mechanical techniques**—Capital letters, bold print, large fonts, underlining, color, and clip art can be used.
- **Space**—The amount of space devoted to developing an idea indicates the amount of emphasis given that idea.
- **Isolation**—The white space around an idea can be used for emphasis.
- **Sentence structure**—Simple sentences are direct and emphatic. Complex and compound sentences are less emphatic than simple sentences.
- **Language**—Specific language is more emphatic than general language.
- **Position**—The first and last sentences are the key emphasis positions in a paragraph.

3

TEST SOLUTIONS

I. Short Answer

1. People like to hear good news; therefore, it is logical to present the good news first. Presenting goods news first helps create a good impression and sets the tone for the entire message. Another psychological advantage is that the direct approach uses emphasis techniques effectively.

2. The strategy for neutral messages begins with the most important news to be conveyed, whereas the positive message begins with the good news that must be conveyed. Otherwise the same strategy is used for both types of messages.

3. By analyzing both your needs and those of the reader and by making all decisions, you can determine the strategy that will best meet your needs and those of the reader. Positive decisions that will please the reader call for a different writing strategy than do negative decisions that will displease the reader.

4. Global communications may require language translation. Translations often do not convey the meaning or tone that was intended. Differences in culture also create major challenges. People in different countries respond differently to the same information. Distributing information to remote locations in different time zones also presents challenges.

5. Stereotyped messages sound alike. Planning messages carefully so that they are specifically designed to meet the objectives of a particular reader prevents stereotyped messages.

II. Problems

1. You wish to ensure that Trinity will be at the Awards Banquet but that she will not be told in advance that she is the Female Athlete of the Year.

2. Ms. Massa has the same objectives that you do. She wants to ensure that her athlete will be available to receive the award.

3. You know that Ms. Massa cared enough about the award to spend the time necessary to put together a winning nomination package. You also know that athletic directors actively seek awards for student athletes because it is good for their program.

4. You should present the good news first because it will be well received and will set a positive tone for the entire letter.

5. Outline

   A. Announce and congratulate the winner.
   B. Point out the importance of attending the banquet.
   C. Ensure that the recipient is not told about the final outcome.
   D. Refer to the brochure containing all the logistical information.
   E. Thank Ms. Massa for the nomination and close on a goodwill note.

 National Athletic Conference Awards Selection Committee
3702 SE Cedar Street • Portland, OR 97201-5374 • 503-555-0103

Current date

Ms. Susan Massa, Athletics Director
The Bass Athletics Center
Central State University
3284 Hunter Avenue
Brooklyn, NY 11214-8639

Dear Ms. Massa

Congratulations! Trinity Lee has been selected as the Female Athlete of the Year. This is an outstanding achievement for Trinity, the softball program, and for your entire athletics program at Central State University.

Trinity should be informed only that she is a finalist and that it is very important to be at the banquet. You and the Committee are the only individuals who will know the final results until Trinity is announced as the Female Athlete of the Year at the Awards Banquet. The enclosed brochure contains all the logistical details needed to make reservations and attend the banquet.

Thank you, Ms. Massa, for preparing an excellent nomination. We look forward to an exciting Awards Banquet.

Sincerely

Student's name, Chair
Awards Selection Committee

pr

Enclosure: brochure

Test 3, III

TEST SOLUTIONS

I. Short Answer

1. A mixed-news message contains both good and bad news, whereas a bad-news message contains only bad news.

2. A good buffer is a neutral statement that enables the writer to explain the situation logically before presenting negative news. A good buffer allows you to establish that you have acted in a logical, fair, and reasonable manner. It does not mislead the reader into thinking good news may follow.

3. The strategy for writing a mixed-news message is to present the good news first and then explain the negative portion of the message. In a bad news message, you have no good news to present; therefore, you should begin with a buffer that allows you to explain the situation.

4. A direct style would be appropriate because the situation concerns a product problem, and most people welcome information that enables them to correct the problem and maintain the business.

5. The following techniques can be used to de-emphasize negative information:

   - **Mechanical techniques**—Use attributes that do not attract attention and avoid bold print, capital letters, underlining, and large fonts.
   - **Space**—Limit the amount of space devoted to the negative information.
   - **Isolation**—Ensure that negative information is not surrounded by white space.
   - **Sentence structure**—Use compound and complex sentences rather than simple, emphatic sentences.
   - **Language**—Use general language and passive voice rather than specific language and active voice.
   - **Position**—Place negative material in the middle sentences of paragraphs and the middle paragraphs of letters and memos.

II. Letter

Eagles Ticket Office
W.C. Wexford Athletics Center
2846 Kingston Road • Amarillo, TX 79106-3275
(606) 555-0109

Current date

Ms. Connie Marshall
7654 Moss Lane
Amarillo, TX 79109-7284

Dear Ms. Marshall

Providing each Eagle fan with the best football seats available is my goal
as ticket manager. Therefore, when I received your letter, I reviewed it and
our seat availability very carefully to determine if there was any way
possible to upgrade your seats.

Based on an agreement with our Eagle booster club, we make seat
assignments on a priority system with points based on sustained contribution
levels. Club seats are provided only for Golden Eagle contributors. Prime
seats (those between the 40- and 50-yard lines in the east stands) are
provided first to full-scholarship donors with priority based on the number of
years the fan has provided a full scholarship. Prime seats in the west stands
are reserved for faculty and students. Currently, we have a waiting list of
full-scholarship donors desiring prime seats; therefore, it will not be possible
to assign your seats in this area.

Your sustained level of contribution qualifies you for the next level of
seats—those between the 20-and 40-yard lines. We are monitoring your
point status carefully and will upgrade your seats as soon as four seats
become available. We appreciate your support of the Eagles, and we look
forward to a great football season.

Sincerely

Student's name
Ticket Manager

pr

Test IV, II

5

TEST SOLUTIONS

I. Short Answer

1. The two major factors that influence persuasion are the credibility of the writer and the appeal of the message.

   • For the writer to have credibility, the reader must perceive the writer as being knowledgeable, honest, sincere, and in control of the situation. For a message to have credibility, the reader must judge it to be accurate, clear, easy to understand, and supported with adequate information.
   • A message can have either a logical or a psychological appeal. A logical appeal seems reasonable and makes good sense to the reader. A psychological appeal stimulates the reader's emotions and makes the reader feel that the request is a good thing to do.

2. Brainstorming is a technique used to stimulate creative thinking. Persuasion involves selecting the right appeal. Creative thinking is needed to come up with an approach that will appeal to the reader. Brainstorming works to generate as many ideas as possible; then those ideas are checked for credibility.

3. The following strategy is recommended for persuasive messages:

   • Attract the reader's attention and interest.
   • Explain the request carefully, making sure that it is fully justified.
   • Minimize the obstacles and make it as easy as possible for the reader to act.
   • Request the desired action confidently.

4. The following techniques ensure that messages sent to individuals in other countries are easy to interpret:

   • Use a simple, straightforward writing style.
   • Use concrete language.
   • Use standard English and avoid slang, idioms, and expressions that may be difficult to translate.
   • Use bulleted items, charts, graphs, and illustrations to simplify data.
   • Use familiar words, short sentences, and short paragraphs to make the document more readable.

5. Persuasive techniques that intimidate, manipulate, misrepresent, mislead, or take advantage of someone else are inappropriate and may be considered unethical.

II. Letter

Bradley Technical Academy
2938 Mountain View Drive • Castle Rock, CO 80104-3746
(303) 555-0109

Current date

Ms. Amy Posten
2838 Sandhurst Drive
Castle Rock, CO 80104-6201

Dear Ms. Posten

Excellent communication skills are critical for success in virtually every career. Unfortunately, many of our students have not had the opportunity to develop their communication skills appropriately. Employers find it difficult to hire young people whose communication skills are not adequate to meet job requirements.

Bradley Technical Academy is committed to helping our community solve this problem. Our plan is to establish a Business Communication Center to provide assistance to students who need help in improving their writing and speaking skills. Facilities are available for the Center, but we need to raise approximately $1 million to provide state-of-the-art equipment and personnel to staff the Center.

We are convinced that we can make major progress in solving this problem—with help from you and your friends and associates. You are a very effective fund-raiser, and we hope that you will assist us in making the Business Communication Center a reality. The impact on our students and in the business community will be felt for many years.

We will prepare the proposals. We ask that you help us target the proper individuals and go with us to visit carefully selected potential donors to whom we will submit the proposals. Together we can make a difference in the skills that our students bring to the workplace when they graduate. I will call you later this week to determine your availability for this very worthwhile project.

Sincerely

Student's name, Chair
Business Communication Department

pr

Test 5, II

CHAPTER 6

TEST SOLUTIONS

I. Short Answer

1. Letter format is used for short, relatively simple, informal reports written to individuals outside the company. Memo format is used for short, relatively simple, informal reports written to individuals within the company.

2. Components contain the following information:

   - **Identifying information** includes the title of the report, the name of the person or persons who prepared the report, the individual or group who requested the report, and the date.
   - The **problem statement** explains the purpose of the report.
   - **Supporting data** consist of information collected to solve the problem.
   - The **data analysis** is a discussion of the facts and an interpretation of how those facts can be used to solve the problem.
   - The **conclusions** are the results obtained by analyzing and interpreting the facts.
   - The **recommendations** are suggested courses of action based on the conclusion.
   - The **summary** is a brief synopsis of the report explaining what was done, how it was done, and the results.

3. An indirect organizational approach should be used so that the reasons for the conclusion can be presented and justified prior to presenting the conclusion. The reader is more likely to receive the supporting information objectively if it is presented before the conclusion is known.

4. Objective style is preferable because it gives the appearance that the conclusion is based on fact rather than on an individual's opinion.

5. A regular summary is a brief synopsis of the report presented at the end of the report or combined with the conclusions and recommendations. An executive summary is a stand-alone briefing presented at the beginning of the report.

VanHuss Industries, Inc.

TO: Mary Jeffcoat, Vice President of Operations

FROM: Student's name

DATE: Current date

SUBJECT: Lawn Proposal

The purpose of this report was to determine the cost and best method of establishing a lawn on the 2.5-acre lot surrounding our new building. Bids were provided by five reputable companies on which we received good references. Copies of the bids are attached.

Of the five companies submitting bids, Green Acres provided the lowest cost bid. Green Acres offered a choice of three options: hydro-seeding, sprigging, and rolling out sod. The following chart shows the comparative costs of the options:

Options	Cost	Expected Results
Hydro-seeding	$ 7,500	Acceptable lawn first year; top-quality lawn in second growing season
Sprigging	$11,000	Very good quality lawn in one year
Sod	$21,000	Top-quality lawn within one to two months

The appearance of our property, the impact on our customers, and our company image were also considered. In its public relations materials, VanHuss Industries promotes its image of stability and its 60-year history of outstanding service in the community. Therefore, time required to establish a quality lawn was given major consideration. Convenience to customers was also given major weight in the decision process.

Although rolling out sod is the most expensive option, it appears to be the best option because it is the only one that provides a high-quality lawn in a short period of time. A poorly established lawn would conflict with our image. It would also be an inconvenience to customers trying to get from the parking area to the building because of the extensive watering required to establish a new lawn. My recommendation is to have sod rolled out as quickly as possible.

Test 6, II

CHAPTER

7

TEST SOLUTIONS

I. Short Answer

1. Form messages are used for situations in which similar messages are sent to multiple individuals. Forms should be used only when they are both effective and efficient. Effective means that the form meets the needs of the reader, and efficient means that time is saved in producing the messages.

2. A complete form is a printed message that is sent to many individuals without any customization whatsoever. A guide form is a sample that is used to prepare an individual message for each recipient.

3. Word processing software makes it easy to produce form messages very quickly. Databases, address books, and spreadsheets can be linked so that information from multiple sources can be merged automatically. Technology has also enhanced the distribution of form messages.

4. A variable form is a letter or memo with minor variations in content that are inserted for each individual message. Form paragraphs are a series of paragraphs designed for specific situations. The message is prepared by selecting the appropriate beginning, middle, and end paragraphs to meet the needs of the situation.

5. Electronic form messages can be sent over the Internet. Distribution lists for complete forms are a very common use of electronic form messages.

Pommery Medical Center
4854 Arnold Lane · Hopkins, SC 29016 · (803) 555-0108

Brooke Paynter, MD

August 15, 1999

Mr. Richard McKay
4859 Tom's Creek Road
Hopkins, SC 29061

Dear Mr. McKay

This letter confirms your office visit at 10:30 a.m. on Friday, August 22, 1999. Parking is now available in the new lot adjoining our building. The entrance to the parking area is located on Garners Ferry Road. Please report to the desk at the main entrance as soon as you arrive.

Please call the office if you have any questions about your pending visit.

Sincerely

Brooke Paynter, MD

pr

Test 7, II–2

Pommery Medical Center
4854 Arnold Lane · Hopkins, SC 29016 · (803) 555-0108

Brooke Paynter, MD

<Date>

<Title> <FirstName> <LastName>
<Street Address>
<City>, SC <PostalCode>

Dear <Title> <LastName>

This letter confirms your <Type> at <Time> on <Day>, <Date>. Parking is now available in the new lot adjoining our building. The entrance to the parking area is located on Garners Ferry Road. Please report to the desk at the main entrance as soon as you arrive.

Please call the office if you have any questions about your pending visit.

Sincerely

Brooke Paynter, MD

pr

Test 7, II–1

TEST SOLUTIONS

I. Short Answer

1. An individual working on a project can do the project the way he or she feels it should be done. When a team works on a project, team members may have different perspectives about how the project should be done. Agreement has to be reached on how the project is done and on how to produce a written document, if required, that looks like one person wrote it.

2. A team usually can produce better results because of the synergy that comes from different people bringing in different ideas or perspectives. One person may not think of all the aspects that a team will consider.

3. A team consensus is important if a document is to look as though one person wrote it. Careful planning of content, stylistic elements, and format is necessary. Content issues that must be decided on are

   • the level of detail
   • the style of writing—active vs. passive
   • how sections will open and close so that they fit together and flow smoothly

   Mechanical issues that must be considered are

   • font, font size, margins, and general layout
   • type of headings and style in which they are formatted
   • use of italics or underlining for titles
   • use of headers and footers
   • pagination style

4. The key word processing features that facilitate group writing are annotations, revisions, redlining, and comments. These features allow different people to suggest changes to be made in the document. The originator of the document can then decide to accept or reject the suggested changes.

5. Groupware is software that allows a team to manage a document. Members of the team can access the document and send comments about it to a central point. The entire group has access to the comments and can respond to them. Members can be in remote locations and still access the document.

II. Team Project

   Solutions may vary significantly. See following for an acceptable example.

GUIDES FOR PREPARING EFFECTIVE VISUAL AIDS

Visuals are designed to facilitate communication. Good visuals help clarify messages and make them easier to understand. Good visuals also speed up the delivery of the message and enhance retention.

1. LIMIT THE NUMBER OF DESIGN ELEMENTS AND USE THEM CONSISTENTLY

- Use titles, subtitles, captions, graphics, shaded backgrounds, bullets, and other design elements consistently to provide structure.
- Use white space generously to enhance readability.
- Use ragged right margins to avoid adding spaces within lines of text.
- Use wide margins (1.5 inches; 5 or 6 words per line).
- Limit the number of lines of copy on each transparency (6 to 8 per transparency).
- Use spacing consistently.
- Select the font carefully.
- Use a sans serif typeface (plain type with large, open letters).
- Use bold type to enhance readability.
- Vary the size of the typeface (extra large, very large, large) to indicate importance of different levels of headings.
- Use large point sizes. Type smaller than 14 points in charts and graphs usually is not legible when projected; 18-point type is very readable for text; 24-point type provides emphasis for titles.
- Leave space between lines of text.

2. USE A CONSISTENT STYLE

- Use ALL CAPITALS only for titles; upper and lower case letters are easier to read than ALL CAPITALS.
- Use line draw rather than automatic underlining to provide space between text and underline; minimize the use of underlining.
- Indent copy consistently.
- Use bullets rather than numbers when sequence is not important.

3. USE COLOR EFFECTIVELY

Color used functionally is more powerful than black and white in clarifying messages and making them easier to understand. Color also speeds up the delivery of the message and enhances retention.

4. UNDERSTAND THE LANGUAGE OF COLOR

- Recognize that color often connotes meaning within a particular culture

Red	stop, danger, hot, flamboyant
Black	death, somberness, dignity, sophistication
White	pure, clean, sterile
Blue	calm, cool, conservative, reliable
Green	natural, serene, safe
Yellow	bright, cheerful, animated
Pink	feminine
Brown	masculine

Test 8, II

- Be aware of factors that influence color perception.
- Color projected on the screen may not match laser-printed color. Technical charts (such as Pantone® Matching System) are the only reliable way to specify color for identity purposes, such as a company logo.
- Backgrounds influence color; light colors on a dark background appear lighter, and dark colors on a light background appear darker.
- Color is affected by light; differences exist in natural light and fluorescent light.
- Bright colors appear to be larger than dark colors.

5. SELECT AND USE COLORS EFFECTIVELY

- Limit the number of colors; for text visuals, use a maximum of four colors (plus white).
- Select colors that match the purpose and formality of the document.
- Use a light background and dark print to enhance readability; black print on a white background is the most readable print.
- Use larger fonts for color.
- Avoid using pale colors on projected visuals.
- Color code elements of visuals to show linkages.
- Apply color consistently.
- Limit the use of reverse type; reverse type is not as readable as regular type.
- Use bright, saturated colors for important points.
- Avoid using color to bias statistics, such as using bright colors to make one item look larger than other items.
- Make sure that adjacent colors are easy to distinguish from each other.

Test 8, II

TEST SOLUTIONS

I. Short Answer

1. Personal business messages are written primarily to build goodwill. They also should meet the specific objective of the message, such as to convey thanks or appreciation. Just as you want to establish good personal relationships with friends, you want to establish good business relationships with associates with whom you do business.

2. A thank you message is written when someone does something other than that which is expected in ordinary business. Thank you notes would be appropriate if you were

   • invited to a meal, reception, or other function
   • provided a gift, service, or special business opportunity
   • provided a reference or special business contact

3. E-mail is appropriate for informal personal messages such as invitations to casual events, congratulatory notes when you want to distribute copies to others, and internal thank you notes. Script font may be used to prepare some personal business notes.

4. A thank you note should be short, sincere, specific, warm, and friendly.

5. An appropriate sympathy card may be the best way to acknowledge the death of a spouse of a casual business acquaintance. A short note could be added if desired.

II. Thank You Message

VanHuss Industries, Inc.
4820 Forrest Drive • Albany, NY
12205-6927 • (518) 555-0104

Current date

Ms. Carmen Balero
Business Editor
The Business Times
P.O. Box 2058
Albany, NY 12205-2058

Dear Ms. Balero

The feature article you wrote in the Business Section of this past Sunday's Business Times was wonderful. Albany is fortunate to have many excellent companies who support the community. We were pleased to be included in the article, and we especially appreciate the nice comments you made about the financial support VanHuss Industries provides and about the participation of our employees in community activities.

We take great pride in our community. Thank you for the recognition you gave us.

Sincerely

Student's name
President

ms

TEST SOLUTIONS

10

I. Short Answer

1. The first step is to analyze yourself so you know exactly what you have to offer and what you really want to do. Consider what you like to do and what you do not like to do. Examine your strengths and weaknesses and try to decide what type of job utilizes your strengths and minimizes your weaknesses. This self analysis will help you identify good "job matches," prepare effective job-search documents (such as résumés), and prepare for interviews.

2. You should network and try to tap on sources that have access to the hidden job market. Talk with instructors, family, neighbors, friends, and business associates. Check professional journals in the field in which you are interested. Use the Internet and any other sources of information you can locate. A broad search is more likely to uncover opportunities than is a search of ads and placement agencies.

3. Most large companies manage the employment process electronically. They use applicant tracking systems, and they store résumés electronically.

4. You should prepare your résumé in a form that is conducive to electronic scanning. Use nouns so that you will match the keyword search used to screen résumés initially. Use an attractive but simple format that will scan easily. Avoid serif fonts, symbols, clip art, and vertical lines. Make sure your name is the only thing on the top line of your résumé.

5. Because you do not have a person's name as a contact, you need to do research to establish a contact. You can check the company's annual report and publications, the Internet, and current business journals to find articles about the company that include names of people you can use as a contact point.

II. Letter of Application

Student's Name
1000 Main Street
City, State, Postal Code
Telephone Number

Current date

Mr. Antwan Watts
Manager of Human Resources
PO Box 2050
Columbia, SC 29201

Dear Mr. Watts

Last summer as an intern in the Human Resources Division of VanHuss Industries, I had an opportunity to learn about many areas of VanHuss Industries. I also learned that you seek hard working individuals who have the skills needed to do the job and who will continue to grow on the job.

This semester I am completing my studies in Marketing and would like to begin my career as a sales trainee with VanHuss Industries. The knowledge I gained of VanHuss products last summer would give me a head start and allow me to concentrate on applying the sales and marketing skills I learned in school. The enclosed résumé provides additional information about the preparation I have had for a sales and marketing career.

The rating that my supervisor, Ms. Heide Sergios, submitted to my instructor coordinating the internship was outstanding. I know that I can also be an outstanding sales trainee. May I come in and talk with you about how I can be that hard working individual who has the skills to be an excellent sales trainee and who will continue to grow on the job?

Sincerely

Student's name

Enclosure: résumé

Solution Test 9, II

POSTTEST SOLUTIONS

I. Guides for Writing

1. The supplies you ordered were shipped as soon as your payment for the past due account was received.

2. Please revise the report and include the financial analysis we discussed.

3. Our sales representative will ask a secretary in the Small Appliance Division for an appointment with one of the managers at a convenient time.

4. Please secure my approval on a request before asking for the president's approval.

5. The copy of the Asset Allocation Report you requested is being sent today by priority mail.

6. Crystal Clear Pools built the swimming pool, and Mike's Pool Service maintains it.

7. Pat paid $38,000 for a 50-foot-long swimming pool that holds 45,000 gallons of water.

8. I was vacuuming the house when the telephone rang, and I missed your call.

9. The conference call has been rescheduled for April 3, and the new date has been posted on your calendar.

10. Professor Russell Halkyard made the presentation, and Class President Amy Westfield delivered the response.

II. Short Answer

1. The following techniques can be used to emphasize information:

- Mechanical—Using a large font and attributes such as bold and italic type, capital letters, and underlining provides emphasis.
- Space—Devoting a large amount of space to an item emphasizes it.
- Isolation—Using white space around an idea adds emphasis to it.
- Sentence structure—Using a simple, direct sentence provides emphasis.

- Language—Using specific language is more emphatic than using general language.
- Position—Placing information in the first and last sentences or paragraphs gives it more emphasis than burying it in the middle.

2. A good strategy for writing persuasive messages is to

- attract the reader's attention and interest
- explain the request carefully, making sure that it is fully justified
- minimize the obstacles and make it as easy as possible for the reader to act
- request the desired action confidently.

3. Four organizational approaches used for reports are

- narrative—gives an account of events in the sequence they occurred
- direct, or deductive—presents the conclusion or key information first and then provides the supporting details.
- indirect, or inductive—presents supporting information first and then lets those facts lead to the conclusion.
- weighted—presents information in the order of importance and then concludes with a summary of the most important information.

4. Four types of form messages that can be used to make document preparation more efficient are

- complete forms—identical letters or memos that are printed and sent to multiple recipients
- variable forms—documents with minor variations that are filled in and can be sent to multiple recipients
- Form paragraphs—documents constructed by selecting paragraphs from a series of prewritten beginning, middle, and ending paragraphs
- Guide forms—samples or models that can be used as guides for preparing similar documents

5. The following planning steps should be taken before writing a bad-news message:

- Verify and justify the decision carefully before conveying bad news.
- Determine the severity and the sensitivity of the situation to determine how to handle it.
- Decide on the best media to convey the bad news.
- Determine who should convey the news if it is serious.

The following steps are used in writing the bad-news message:

- Be tactful and sincere.
- Prepare the reader.
- Use empathy.
- Analyze the situation carefully to select the best style.

Student's Name
28 Olde Stream Court
Irmo, SC 29063-7362
(803) 555-0109

Current date

Ms. Marge McCants
Human Resources Associate
VanHuss Industries
1043 Spruce Street
Boulder, CO 80302-5893

Dear Ms. McCants

Thank you for the wonderful hospitality you provided during my visit to VanHuss Industries. I especially appreciate the preview that you gave me the first evening at dinner. The information you provided helped me prepare for the interviews and really got me excited about the possibility of working for VanHuss Industries. I enjoyed the evening and the delicious dinner very much.

I also appreciated the opportunity to meet with a number of managers and employees. They convinced me even more that VanHuss Industries is the company in which I would like to begin my career. Boulder is a wonderful community, and I was very pleased with the tour provided by the real estate agent.

I look forward to hearing from you, and I hope you will give me the opportunity to demonstrate that I can be an excellent financial analyst for VanHuss Industries.

Sincerely

Student's name

Solution Test 10 III–2

The Community Foundation
PO Box 1089 • Magnolia, MS 39652-1089
(601) 555-0103

Current date

Mr. Mickey Marx, Owner
The Marx Company
PO Box 2867
Magnolia, MS 39652-5893

Dear Mr. Marx

The Executive Committee of The Community Foundation reviewed the designs and proposals to prepare the Community Foundation Annual Report that were submitted by the three companies who responded to the bid request. The criteria used for selection were design and price.

Two of the companies—your company and the Cox Company—submitted excellent designs. Your bid, however, was more than $20,000 higher than the bid submitted by the Cox Company; therefore, the bid was awarded to the Cox Company.

We appreciate your submitting an excellent proposal and bid, and we hope to have the opportunity to do business with you in the future.

Sincerely

Student's name
Director

pr

Solution Test 10 III–1

Factors Influencing Mode of Communication

- Anticipated response of recipient
- Sensitivity of the situation
- Speed required
- Need for documentation
- Destination and accessibility of the recipient
- Costs involved

CHAPTER 1

Cost Determinants

- Who produces the document

- Where the document is produced

- How the document is produced

- What type of document is produced

CHAPTER 1

Ten Guides for Effective Writing

- Plan messages carefully
- Write for the reader
- Present ideas positively
- Write in a clear, readable style
- Check for completeness

Ten Guides for Effective Writing

- Use an efficient, action-oriented style
- Use concrete language
- Use effective sentence and paragraph structure
- Format documents effectively
- Edit and proofread carefully

Planning Messages

- Determine objectives
- Analyze the reader
- Make decisions
- Collect information
- Develop the plan

CHAPTER 2

Guides for E-Mail Messages

- ■ Use short line length
- ■ Keep paragraphs short
- ■ Limit documents to one page
- ■ Avoid special characters
- ■ Use concise writing style
- ■ Avoid cryptic messages and sarcasm

CHAPTER 2

Planning Good-News Messages

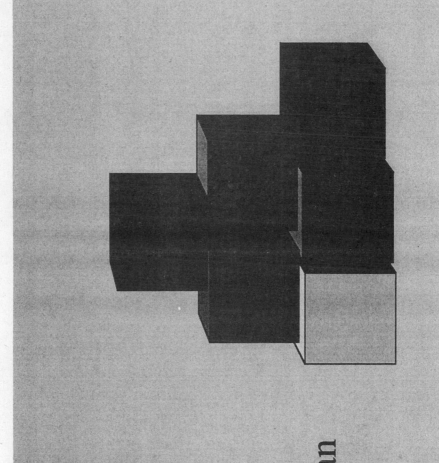

- ■ Determine objectives
- ■ Analyze the reader
- ■ Make decisions
- ■ Collect information
- ■ Develop a writing plan
- ■ Implement the plan

Strategy for Good-News Messages

- Present good news early
- Provide supporting details
- Close on a friendly note

Strategy for Neutral Messages

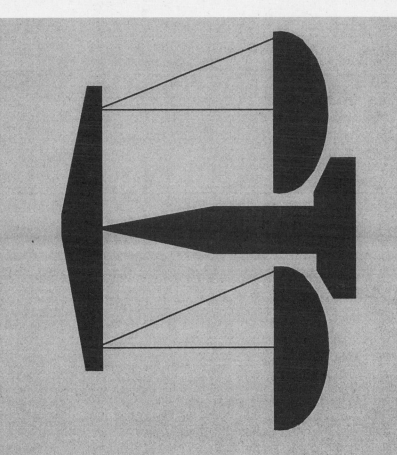

- Present most important information first

- Provide supporting details

- Close with a positive, friendly paragraph

Planning Bad-News Messages

- Verify and justify the decision
- Determine the sensitivity of the situation
- Decide on best media to convey bad news
- Determine who should convey the bad news
- Be tactful and sincere
- Prepare the reader
- Use empathy
- Analyze the situation carefully

CHAPTER 4

Strategy for Bad-News Messages

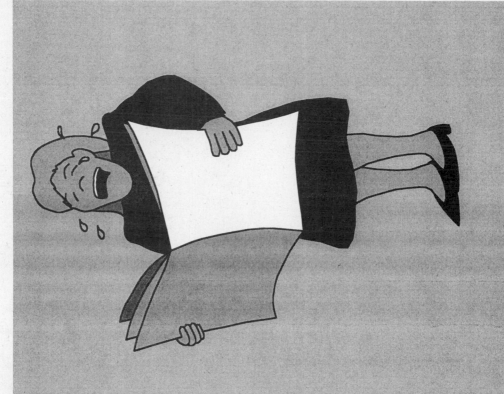

- Begin with a buffer
- Explain the reasons for your decisions
- Present your refusal
- Offer helpful suggestions if appropriate
- Close on a positive note

CHAPTER 4

Strategy for Mixed-News Messages

- Present the good news first
- Explain the reasons for the negative portion
- Let reasons lead to the negative information
- Present the negatives as positively as possible
- Close with a goodwill-building statement

Modified Direct Approach for Mixed News

- Present the problem factually
- Present additional details and justify your request
- Request the action that you desire
- Close on a friendly note

Factors that Influence Persuasion

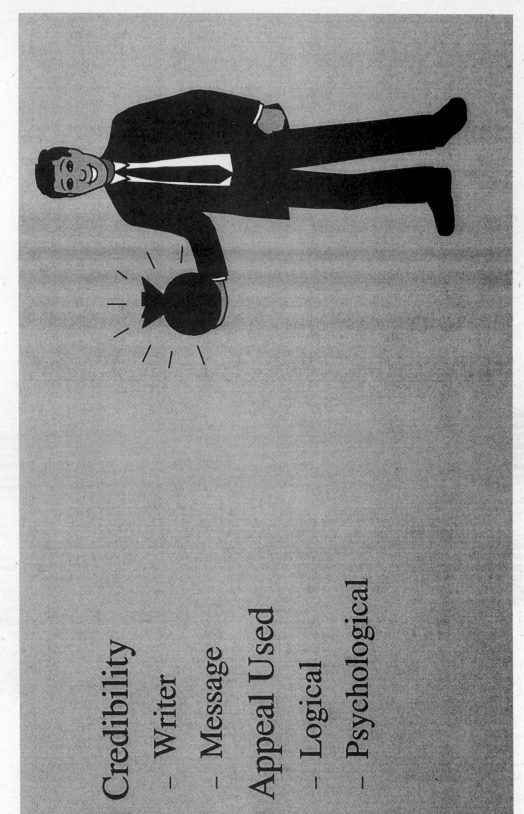

- Credibility
  – Writer
  – Message
- Appeal Used
  – Logical
  – Psychological

Strategy for Writing Persuasive Messages

- ■ Attract the reader's attention and interest
- ■ Explain the request carefully
- ■ Minimize the obstacles
- ■ Request the desired action confidently

CHAPTER 5

Report Content

- Identifying information
- Problem statement
- Supporting data
- Data analysis
- Conclusions
- Recommendations
- Summary

CHAPTER 6

Report Organization

- Narrative style
- Direct, or deductive, style
- Indirect, or inductive, style
- Weighted style

Types of Form Messages

- Complete forms
- Variable forms
- Form paragraphs
- Guide forms

Strategies for Team Writing

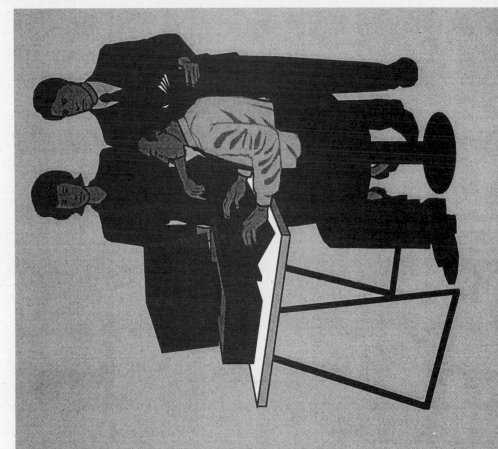

- Content Consistency
  - Level of detail is important
  - Style of writing should be similar
  - Sections should fit together

Strategies for Team Writing

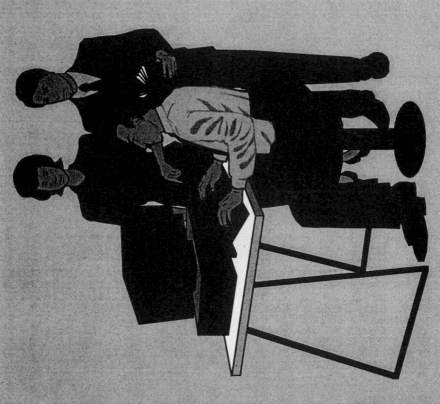

- Mechanical Consistency
  - Font, font size, margins, and general layout
  - Type and format of headings
  - Italics or underlining for titles
  - Headers and footers
  - Pagination

Types of Personal Business Messages

- Thank you messages
- Congratulatory messages
- Special occasion messages
- Sympathy messages

Guides for Electronic Résumés

- Use nouns for key word tracking systems
- Use simple, attractive format
- Use sans serif font
- Avoid vertical lines and clip art

Components of a Résumé

- Identifying information
- Career objectives
- Summary of qualifications
- Education
- Experience
- Honors and activities
- Special skills

Strategies for Writing an Application Letter

- Establish a point of contact
- Specify the type of job you are seeking
- Highlight your major qualifications
- Refer to the resume that you will enclose
- Request an interview